Reader's Digest
Pathfinders

Earthquakes and Volcanoes

Reader's Digest
Children's Books™

Pleasantville, New York • Montréal, Québec

Contents

Dynamic Earth 6

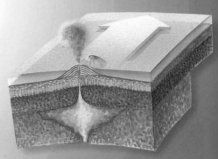

Earthquakes 20

Volcanoes 36

Pick Your Path!

EARTHQUAKES AND VOLCANOES is different from any other information book you've ever read. Start at the beginning and learn about Earth's fiery interior, then read through to the end and find out about volcanoes on other planets. Or, if you have a special interest in earthquakes, jump right into "On Shaky Ground" and move through the book from there.

You'll find plenty of other discovery paths to choose from in the special features sections. Read eyewitness accounts of volcanoes and earthquakes in "Inside Story," or get creative with "Hands On" activities. Delve into words with "Word Builders," or amaze your friends with fascinating facts from "That's Amazing!" You can choose a new path with every reading—READER'S DIGEST PATHFINDERS will take you wherever *you* want to go.

INSIDE STORY
Where the Action Is

Fly over Mount St. Helens as it erupts with geologists Keith and Dorothy Stoffel. Read photographer Carl Mydans' account of a major Japanese earthquake. Learn how postmaster Masao Mimatsu watched a volcano grow before his eyes. Study the shape of the seafloor with oceanographer Harry Hess. Read about great scientists, terrifying tremors, and spectacular eruptions in INSIDE STORY. Imagine you are there, and you will understand how it feels to experience earth-shattering events or discover something that changes our view of the world.

HANDS ON
Shake and Bake

Create a volcanic eruption in your kitchen. Learn about earthquake-proof buildings by making a shake table. Bake a volcano cake that oozes chocolate lava. Construct your own seismometer and use it to record tremors. Use binoculars to study ancient lava flows on the surface of the Moon. HANDS ON features experiments, projects, and activities—each one related to that page's main subject.

Word Builders

What a strange word! What does it mean? Where did it come from? Find out by reading *Word Builders*.

That's Amazing!

Awesome facts, amazing records, fascinating figures— you'll find them all in *That's Amazing!*

Pathfinder

Use the *Pathfinder* section to find your way from one subject to another. It's all up to you.

Ready! Set! Start exploring!

Dynamic Earth

TREMORS AND EXPLOSIONS constantly rock our planet. Most of these earthly hiccups are caused by the shifting of rocks in the ground. These movements, in turn, are powered by heat from Earth's core. The heat causes some of the rock between the core and the surface to rise and sink like currents in hot water. This circulation constantly tugs at the crust and, over millions of years, has broken it into pieces, or plates. The plates slowly pull apart, collide, and grind past each other. When a plate shifts suddenly, we feel the movement as an earthquake. If the rock below a plate melts, the liquid rock may spurt out of the ground, forming a volcano.

page **14** What happens when sections of the crust collide?

A collision between which two continents created the largest mountain range on Earth?

Go to **COLLISIONS**.

page **16** When rock layers move in different directions, faults form. What type of fault is this?

Some types of faults create distinctive landforms. What's this landform called?

Go to **FAULT LINES**.

page **18** Did you realize that this island is the top of a volcano?

How can you make your own chain of volcanoes?

Go to **HOT SPOTS**.

The interior of the Moon

The interior of Mars

The interior of Venus

EARTH'S LAYERS
Earth is a bit like a boiled egg. The crust is the shell, the mantle is the stiff white, and the core is the yolk.

Crust
3–43 miles
(5–70 km) thick

Mantle
1,800 miles
(2,900 km) thick

Outer core
1,400 miles
(2,250 km) thick

Inner core
750 miles
(1,200 km) thick

Heart of Fire

LOOK DOWN at the ground. Have you ever wondered what lies beneath your feet? Did you know that you live on a huge ball of rock? No one can travel to the center of this giant rock because the heat and pressure inside our planet are so great that even the toughest drills would melt just 8 miles (13 km) below the surface. But if you could go on such a trip, this is what you would find.

First, you would pass through a layer of rocks called the crust. The crust is thicker under land than it is under the ocean. At its thinnest, the crust is only 3 miles (5 km) deep. You could walk that far in an hour. However, the thickest part of the crust is 43 miles (70 km) deep, a distance that would take you at least two days to walk. Beyond the crust, you would enter the mantle. The upper part of the mantle is solid, but the deeper part is soft. The mantle is more than 40 times wider than the thickest part of the crust.

If you could descend through the mantle, you would arrive at the core. The outer part of the core is made of molten iron, but near the center it is solid iron. Earth's center lies about 4,000 miles (6,370 km) below you—a distance that would take about eight hours to travel by plane. Here, in our planet's fiery heart, the temperature is 50 times hotter than that of boiling water, and the pressure is 5 million times greater than the pressure of the air on our bodies at Earth's surface.

IN THE UNDERWORLD
For centuries, people have wondered what lies inside Earth. In the 17th century, a German religion professor named Alhanasius Kircher climbed into a volcano to learn more about the planet's interior. His studies led him to suggest that volcanoes were linked by rivers of lava that sprang from fires within the Earth.

A GROWING PLANET

IN THE BEGINNING
Our solar system emerged from a giant cloud of dust and gas. About 4.6 billion years ago, this cloud started spinning rapidly, pulling hot gases toward its center. These gases formed the Sun. Farther out, pieces of dust and rock collided and bonded to form planets. Earth, the third planet from the Sun, was born about 4.5 billion years ago. The remaining gases and dust were blown out of the solar sytem by a blast of radiation from the Sun.

HEATING UP
While meteorites continuously bombarded Earth, radioactive materials inside the planet began to decay and heat up. Rocks started to melt, and heavy metal materials sank to the center, leaving lighter minerals in the outer part. Shortly after Earth formed, a small planet slammed into it, spraying debris into space. Some of this material spun into a ball, forming the Moon.

Word Builders

• The word **mantle** comes from the Latin word *mantellum,* meaning "cloak" or "cover." The mantle cloaks, or covers, the core.
• As a rock hurtles through space, it is called a **meteoroid**. If it passes through Earth's atmosphere, it is known as a **meteor**. If it reaches the ground, it is called a **meteorite**. All three words come from the Greek *meteoron,* meaning "something high in the sky."

That's Amazing!

• The energy released when Earth formed was so great that it still powers volcanic eruptions after more than 4 billion years of cooling.
• Volcanoes can bring up rocks and minerals from as deep as 375 miles (600 km) below Earth's surface. These materials can include diamonds.
• We know more about distant stars than about the workings of Earth's core.

Pathfinder

• Earth's crust is solid, but it is broken into pieces that constantly move around. Learn more on pages 10–11.
• Movement of Earth's crust is one cause of earthquakes. Read about the biggest quakes in history on pages 30–31.
• Earth isn't the only planet that has earthquakes and volcanoes. Find out more on pages 60–61.

FROM THE HEART

In many parts of the world, red-hot streams of soft, hot rock called magma rise through the crust and emerge on Earth's surface as lava. Scientists study the rock and minerals in lava to learn about our planet's hot interior.

SPACE ROCKS

Meteorites are rocks that crash onto Earth from space. Most come from the asteroid belt, a band of rocky lumps that orbit between Mars and Jupiter. Many are made of iron, much like the rocks at the center of our planet. Scientists study asteroids to learn more about Earth's core.

INSIDE STORY

Watching the Waves

Scientists study Earth's interior by monitoring the shock waves created by big earthquakes. The speed and direction of the waves tell them what kinds of rocks make up Earth's layers. In the 1930s, scientists knew only that Earth had a crust, mantle, and core. Then a Danish scientist named Inge Lehmann began to study earthquakes. A nephew, Niels Groes, recalls that his aunt kept records of the speed of shock waves on cards that she filed in oatmeal boxes. These records showed that some waves changed direction as they passed through the core. Using this information, Lehmann published a paper in 1936 that proposed a possible solid inner core within Earth's outer core.

COOLING OFF

The constant bombardment by meteorites left giant scars and huge oceans of lava on the surfaces of Earth and the Moon. As the lava cooled, it created a hard outer crust on both bodies. Inside Earth, a metallic core formed. By about 3 billion years ago, the Moon was almost completely solid.

SETTLING DOWN

Gradually, the rocks and minerals inside Earth separated into three main layers—the core, mantle, and crust. Volcanoes and meteorites added gases and water to the atmosphere. Oceans began to form, and eventually plants and animals emerged.

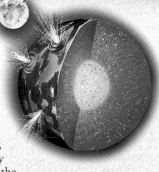

The Shifting Surface

BETWEEN 50 AND 150 MILES (80 and 240 km) below Earth's surface, something strange happens to the rocks of the mantle. They soften, and in places start to melt, forming pockets of molten rock. This creates a weak zone called the asthenosphere. Above the asthenosphere, the solid top of the mantle and crust form a hard shell known as the lithosphere. This shell floats on top of the squishy asthenosphere and slowly moves around.

Because the asthenosphere is soft, its hotter parts rise and begin to cool. Once they have cooled sufficiently, they start to sink again. This rising and sinking creates a kind of circulation called a convection current. These currents constantly push and tug at the lithosphere, breaking Earth's outer shell into pieces called tectonic plates.

Where currents push upward, they force tectonic plates apart. As the plates move, they carry land with them. Over millions of years, moving plates split, forcing continents to collide, and opening and closing oceans. Slowly but surely, this process continues to transform the surface of our planet.

RISING AND FALLING
The East Pacific Rise in the Pacific Ocean is a divergent margin. Here, rising magma pushes the Pacific and Nazca plates outward. Parts of the plates move at different rates, creating cracks called transform faults. The Nazca Plate collides with the South American Plate, forming a convergent margin. Here, the thin ocean plate slides under the continental plate and melts in the mantle.

PUSH AND PULL
The lithosphere is divided into pieces called tectonic plates. These plates have three kinds of margins, or edges. A divergent margin occurs where plates move apart. A convergent margin forms where plates collide. Plates moving past each other create transform fault margins.

Nansen Ridge

EURASIAN PLATE

Reykjanes Ridge

Anatolian Fault

ARABIAN PLATE

AFRICAN PLATE

Mid-Atlantic Ridge

Great Rift Valley

Java Trench

INDO-AUSTRALIAN PLATE

Southwest Indian Ocean Ridge

Southeast Indian Ocean Ridge

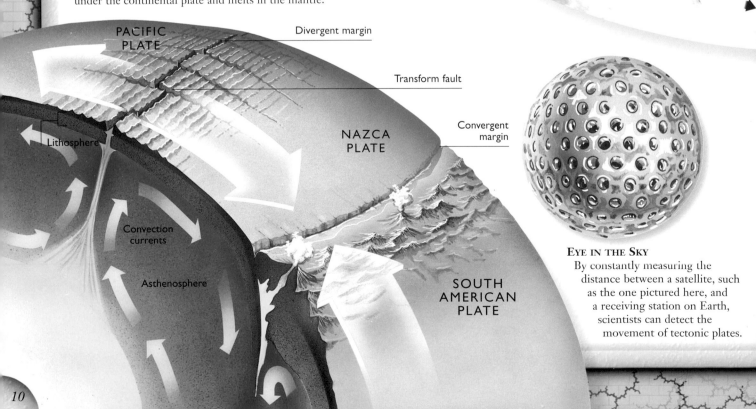

PACIFIC PLATE

Divergent margin

Transform fault

Lithosphere

Convection currents

Asthenosphere

NAZCA PLATE

Convergent margin

SOUTH AMERICAN PLATE

EYE IN THE SKY
By constantly measuring the distance between a satellite, such as the one pictured here, and a receiving station on Earth, scientists can detect the movement of tectonic plates.

Word Builders

• **Lithosphere** comes from the Greek words *lithos,* for "stone," and *sphaira,* for "sphere." The soft **asthenosphere** takes its name from *sphaira* and another Greek word *asthenes,* meaning "weak."
• Buildings and other constructions were called *tektonikos* by the ancient Greeks. In geology, **tectonics** refers to the structures that make up Earth's surface.

That's Amazing!

• Rocks that now lie 6,000 miles (9,660 km) apart, in South America and South Africa, once lay beside each other. They slowly spread apart as a result of the movement of the seafloor.
• The Pacific and Nazca plates are moving apart at the rate of more than 7 inches (18 cm) each year.

Pathfinder

• Diverging plates can create new oceans. To learn how this happens, turn to pages 12–13.
• Plates converge, or collide, in different ways. Turn to pages 14–15.
• Scientists use satellite measurements to predict earthquakes. Find out more on pages 26–27.

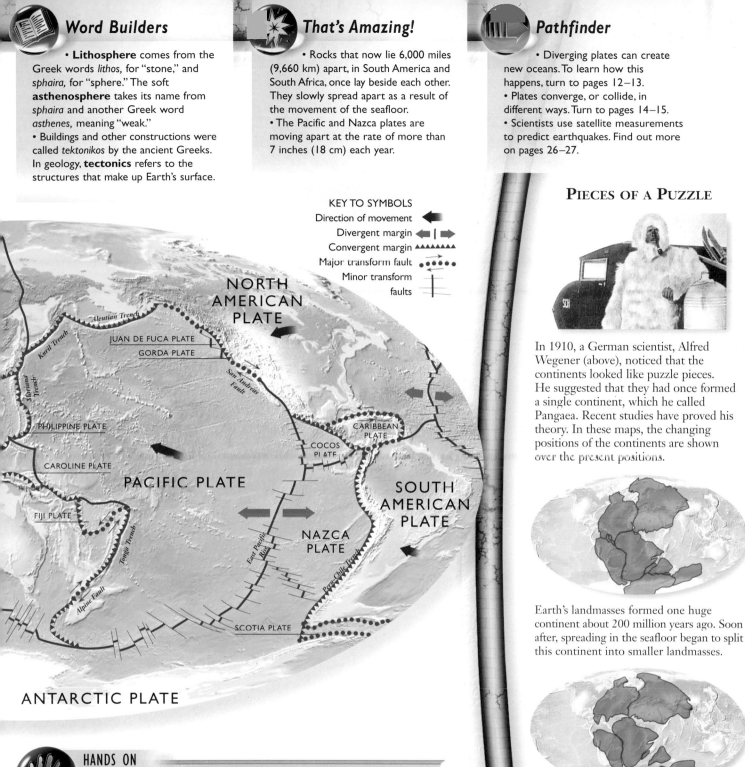

KEY TO SYMBOLS

Direction of movement
Divergent margin
Convergent margin
Major transform fault
Minor transform faults

NORTH AMERICAN PLATE

Aleutian Trench

JUAN DE FUCA PLATE
GORDA PLATE

Kuril Trench

San Andreas Fault

Mariana Trench

PHILIPPINE PLATE

CARIBBEAN PLATE

COCOS PLATE

CAROLINE PLATE

PACIFIC PLATE

SOUTH AMERICAN PLATE

FIJI PLATE

Tonga Trench

East Pacific Rise

NAZCA PLATE

Alpine Fault

Peru-Chile Trench

SCOTIA PLATE

ANTARCTIC PLATE

PIECES OF A PUZZLE

In 1910, a German scientist, Alfred Wegener (above), noticed that the continents looked like puzzle pieces. He suggested that they had once formed a single continent, which he called Pangaea. Recent studies have proved his theory. In these maps, the changing positions of the continents are shown over the present positions.

Earth's landmasses formed one huge continent about 200 million years ago. Soon after, spreading in the seafloor began to split this continent into smaller landmasses.

Spreading in what is now the Atlantic Ocean split North America from Africa 120 million years ago. The widening Indian Ocean pushed India northward.

The Atlantic was already a broad ocean 65 million years ago, and India was on a collision course with the Eurasian Plate.

HANDS ON

Convection Currents

You can see for yourself how convection currents form.

❶ Take a large glass container and fill it with cold water. Fill a smaller jar with hot water and add a few drops of red food coloring.

❷ Cover the top of the small jar with your hand while placing the jar on the bottom of the big container. Take your hand away and watch what happens.

The red water rises toward the top of the cold water and spreads outward. This happens because the red water is hotter than the clear water. As the red water cools, it sinks. This creates a convection current. The same thing happens in Earth's mantle. Hot rock rises toward the lithosphere, then it cools and sinks. As the rock moves, it shifts Earth's tectonic plates.

Cross section of the seafloor of the southern Atlantic Ocean

The Spreading Seas

DEEP BENEATH THE SEAS, massive ridges wend their way along the ocean floors, forming the longest mountain range on Earth. If you could see these ridges from space, they would look like the seams on a giant baseball. Inside the ridges lie huge cracks in the crust. Convection currents in the mantle push magma up through these cracks. Some lava spills out onto the ocean floor and some hardens inside the cracks. As the lava in the cracks cools, it pushes the seafloor outward. Slowly, the plates on either side of the cracks spread, like two conveyor belts moving in opposite directions.

New ocean crust builds up in two layers. Lava that reaches the seafloor cools quickly in the water and forms mounds called pillow lava. Lava that solidifies in the cracks creates vertical sheets called dikes. Beneath the dikes, the mantle forms massive blocks of coarse-grained rock.

It is pitch dark on the ridges, but scientists use various methods to reveal the secrets of this murky world. Ships and satellites bounce laser beams, radar signals, and sonar (sound) waves off the ocean floor to discover its shape. Dredges and drills recover samples of seafloor rocks. And brave explorers descend in submersibles to witness and photograph seafloor spreading in action.

EXPLORING OCEAN RIDGES
Explorers find an eerie world inside ocean ridges. Volcanoes erupt, but the pressure of the seawater keeps these explosions from being felt at the surface. The seafloor bristles with chimneys called black smokers. Mineral-rich water pours out of the chimneys, attracting strange creatures including fish and sea worms.

INSIDE STORY
Spreading the Word

American geologist Harry Hess was the first scientist to explain seafloor spreading. During World War II, he served in submarines, and between battles he studied mountain ranges on the ocean floor. Later, in the 1960s, other scientists revealed that the ocean floor was very thin. Hess realized that molten rock must be constantly oozing up through the thin seafloor to form new crust and mountains. He also suggested that as the seafloor spread outward, it collided with continents and sank back into the mantle. Hess had no way of proving his theory, but scientists have since shown that he was correct.

MAPPING THE SEAFLOOR
Scientists use information from satellites, and from surveys carried out using radar and sonar devices, to create maps of the ocean floor. Here, the ocean ridges are highlighted in pale blue.

PARTING THE LANDSCAPE
Many oceans began life as rift valleys. Rift valleys form where convection currents rise upward, stretching and splitting the crust. As a rift valley widens, water may flood in from a nearby ocean. This creates a new sea that will continue to grow.

RIFTING
When convection currents split the land, faults form. The land tilts and drops, forming a wide valley. Lava may seep through the valley floor.

FLOODING
The hot asthenosphere bulges upward into the fault zone. As the land drops farther, water pours in. Seafloor forms and pushes the landmasses apart.

Word Builders

- By bouncing **radar** and **sonar** signals off the ocean floor, scientists can build up a picture of its shape. The word radar is short for "RAdio Detection And Reading." Sonar is an abbreviation of "SOund NAvigation Ranging."
- **Rift** comes from the Danish word *rift* which means "cleft" or "split."

That's Amazing!

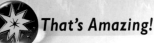

- The Mid-ocean Ridge stretches 48,000 miles (75,000 km) from the Arctic through the Atlantic Ocean, around Africa and Australia, and across the Pacific Ocean to North America.
- In the 1980s, two new species of sea worms, the red-plume worm and the Pompeii worm, were found near black smokers in the Pacific Ocean. The worms live in water that can be three times as hot as boiling water and feed on bacteria.

Pathfinder

- Ocean ridges form where convection currents force magma upward. Learn how to make your own convection currents on page 11.
- Rift valleys are a kind of fault. Discover more about faults on pages 16–17.
- Seafloor spreading is tearing apart the island of Iceland. Turn to pages 56–57.

Black smokers

Pillow lava

Dike

BIRTH OF A SEA
The Red Sea in North Africa started to form 20 million years ago. The process began on land, when rifting created a valley. As the valley widened and deepened, seawater flooded in. Today the Red Sea continues to grow, pushing apart Africa and the Arabian peninsula.

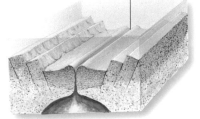

Mid-ocean ridge

SPREADING
As spreading continues, the ocean grows wider. As the seafloor moves outward, it settles and sinks, leaving a high ridge on either side of the rift.

MAGNETIC STRIPES
Like trees, seafloors contain growth bands. As molten rock cools, particles of iron minerals within it line up with Earth's magnetic field like the needle of a compass. Over millions of years, the magnetic field has reversed many times. This has created bands of rock that have either normal magnetism to the north or reverse magnetism to the south. These bands help scientists to date the seafloor and measure its rate of spreading.

▲ Normal magnetism

▼ Reverse magnetism

Mount Augustine, subduction volcano, Alaska, U.S.A.

Mayon, island arc volcano, Philippines

Collisions

TECTONIC PLATES are on collision courses. When they meet, moving plates smash into each other with enormous force. The effects of these collisions depend on the types and thicknesses of the plates involved. When two plates carrying continental crust collide straight on, the land buckles to form large mountain ranges. Plates colliding at a small angle may grind past each other, forming a fault line. In most collisions, however, the duel between the plates is like an arm wrestle, with the thicker, stronger plate forcing the thinner, weaker plate downward. This is called subduction.

Subduction usually occurs when a thin ocean plate meets a thicker ocean plate or continental plate. During subduction, the thicker plate crumples and buckles along the impact zone. This, along with the downward movement of the thinner plate, can trigger earthquakes. As the thinner plate sinks, the mantle heats up and begins to melt. Heat and pressure force the molten rock to the surface where it erupts, forming volcanoes. On land, this usually creates a line of volcanic mountains. When two ocean plates are involved, a chain of volcanic islands called an island arc is formed.

HIGH RISE
The highest mountain range on Earth, the Himalayas in Asia, formed when India collided with Eurasia 60 million years ago. Buckling of the land has made the continental crust here up to 43 miles (70 km) thick.

KINDS OF COLLISION
This cross section shows the three main kinds of plate collisions. On the left, oceanic crust crashes into continental crust, forming subduction volcanoes. In the center, two continents collide, creating a mountain range. On the right, two oceanic plates meet, forming an island arc.

The folding of the continental crust creates a high mountain range.

The process of subduction can form an ocean trench.

Magma rises to the surface and erupts, forming volcanoes.

Subduction zone

WHEN CONTINENTS MEET
After the breakup of Pangaea, India was part of a large southern continent called Gondwana. About 145 million years ago, India broke away and began to drift northward.

About 60 million years ago, India and Eurasia approached each other. India's seafloor began to subduct under Eurasia's, pushing the crust upward and forming a line of volcanoes.

Word Builders

• The word **subduction** comes from two Latin words, *sub,* meaning "under," and *duco,* for "lead." Subduction leads one plate under another.
• The name of the **Himalaya** mountain range comes from the Sanskrit words *hima,* meaning "snow," and *alaya,* meaning "home." For local people, the Himalayas are the home of the snow.

That's Amazing!

• The deepest ocean trench, the Mariana Trench in the Pacific Ocean, is 36,198 feet (11,033 m) deep. That means it could swallow the world's tallest mountain on land, Mount Everest.
• Parts of the Oman Mountains in Arabia were originally seafloor. They formed hundreds of miles away under the Indian Ocean 100 million years ago, but were forced up onto land by plate movements.

Pathfinder

• Collisions occur as oceanic plates spread outward. Learn about seafloor spreading on pages 12–13.
• Plate collisions create shock waves, which in turn cause earthquakes. That's why most quakes occur along plate edges. See pages 30–31.
• Subduction forces magma upward through the crust, where it erupts as lava. Learn about different kinds of volcanic eruptions on pages 38–39.

HANDS ON
Fold Your Own Crust

You can observe how Earth's crust folds and buckles.

① Take several pieces of different-colored modeling clay. Roll the pieces into thin strips and layer the strips on top of each other. Imagine that the pile is part of Earth's crust.

② Place the clay on a smooth surface. Slowly push the ends of the clay inward using your hands or two wooden blocks. Watch what happens.

The clay folds and rises upward in the middle. This is similar to what happens when two continents collide. The crust buckles and folds, rising slowly upward to form mountains.

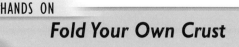

ON THE ARC

Mount Tavurvur, near Rabaul in Papua New Guinea, is an island arc volcano. It lies on a convergent margin between the Pacific and Indo-Australian plates. In 1994, Mount Tavurvur and neighboring Mount Vulcan both erupted violently.

Magma bursts through the crust, forming an arc of volcanic islands.

The thin ocean plate subducts under the thicker ocean plate.

Subduction zone

As the two landmasses pressed together, slices of seabed lying between the continents were thrust upward, forming peaks. Fossil seashells can still be found on top of the Himalayas, tens of thousands of feet above sea level.

As the folding continued, some crust was forced outward, like the bow wave of a ship. This extended the range sideways. The Himalayas are still growing. In the last 3 million years, they have risen 2 miles (3 km).

← *Reverse fault*

Normal fault →

Fault Lines

THE IMMENSE PRESSURES of plate movements snap even the toughest rocks. Cracks between shifting rock layers are called faults. You can see small faults in rock faces, riverbanks, and road cuts. Large faults may extend for hundreds of miles.

Small or large, the type of fault that forms depends on the way the rocks move. When rocks pull apart, one side slips downward. This is called a normal fault. When rocks push together, one side usually rides up over the other, creating a reverse fault. Sometimes rocks slide past each other in opposite directions or at different speeds. This creates a fault called a lateral, or transform, fault. All three kinds of movement may occur along a major fault line.

Large faults shape the landscape in particular ways. Normal faults create long cliffs. A sunken block of land called a rift valley may form between two normal faults. Reverse faults create mountains with a stacked-up or notched look. Low-angle reverse faults, called thrust faults, form wide, low ranges of hills or peaks. Lateral faults may bring different types of rock alongside each other, creating an obvious line in exposed ground. The movement of plates along large faults causes many earthquakes. As the plates press in opposite directions, there may be a sudden release of tension. This jolts the ground, setting off shock waves.

TAKE THE FAULT TEST
Small faults show up best in layered rocks. In this picture, can you tell which side dropped down, by how much, and on what sort of fault? If you said the left side dropped by about an arm's length, and that it's a normal fault, then you're getting the hang of this!

PASSING PLATES
The San Andreas Fault stretches 650 miles (1,046 km) through California in the United States. From an airplane, the fault is clearly visible for most of its length. On the western side, the Pacific Plate grinds slowly northwest. On the eastern side, the North American Plate slides southeast. In the last 150 million years, the plates have moved 350 miles (563 km) in opposite directions.

LARGE-SCALE FAULTS

LATERAL FAULTS
Giant lateral faults can create long grooves in the landscape by placing different types of rock alongside each other. Sometimes folding along the fault forms low mountains. Major lateral faults include the San Andreas (U.S.A.), Atacama (Chile), and Philippine faults.

Lateral fault

Reverse faults

REVERSE FAULTS
On a large scale, reverse faulting can create mountain ranges. As one plate pushes against the other, parts of the crust crack and tilt. As they compress, the blocks of land rise upward. The resulting mountains have a steep face on one side and a shallower incline on the other.

Word Builders

When land drops down between two normal faults, the valley floor is called a **graben**. *Graben* is a German word that means "ditch." A high block left between two grabens is called a **horst**. *Horst* is also a German word and means "eyrie"—the kind of nest that birds of prey build on mountaintops or cliffs.

That's Amazing!

• On the Alpine Fault in New Zealand, the 1-billion-year-old rocks of the Australian Plate now lie alongside 300-million-year-old rocks on the Pacific Plate. The rocks were once hundreds of miles apart but were gradually brought together as a result of movement along the fault.
• Within 30 million years, the eastern side of the Great Rift Valley will probably separate from the rest of Africa, forming a new island and ocean.

Pathfinder

• There are major fault lines in many parts of the world. Find out if one lies near you on pages 10–11.
• Plate movements along the San Andreas Fault have caused many major earthquakes in California. Read more about them on pages 32–33.
• Have you ever experienced an earthquake? Discover what it feels like on pages 22–23.

GREAT RIFT VALLEY

Plate movements are slowly tearing eastern Africa apart. Rising currents have created an enormous fault called the Great Rift Valley. It extends 2,500 miles (4,025 km) from the Red Sea to Mozambique. The valley contains many volcanoes and hot springs.

HANDS ON
Cake Movements

You can use a layer cake to understand fault movements.

1. Buy or make a rectangular layer cake, preferably one that is not too soft or messy. Cut the cake in half and then cut one half into quarters. Place the quarters on a flat base and push them in opposite directions. This is a lateral fault.

2. Take the other half of the cake and cut through it at an angle. Follow the diagrams at the top of the opposite page to make a normal and a reverse fault. Practice until you know which fault is which. Then you can eat your cake!

RIFT VALLEYS

When a continent is pulled apart by opposing plate movements, parallel faults form. The land between the faults may collapse, forming a wide valley called a rift valley. The steep walls of the valley are known as fault scarps, and the sunken land is called a graben.

Rift valley

Thrust faults

THRUST FAULTS

Thrust faults form when plate movements push a layer of rock across the top of another layer at a low angle. Here, subduction has thrust part of the seafloor over the continent. Similar processes created the Japan Alps and the Appalachian Mountains in the U.S.A.

Bora-Bora, French Polynesia
(10 million years old)

Lord Howe Island, Australia
(7 million years old)

Molokini, Hawaii,
U.S.A. (4,000 years old)

Hot Spots

AT MANY PLACES and times in Earth's history, a region of hotter rock, called a hot spot, has formed deep in the mantle. This hot rock rises, forming a column called a thermal plume. The plume material melts to form magma, which moves up through the lithosphere like a blowtorch, forcing lava onto the surface and forming a volcano.

Because plates are always on the move, hot spots usually create chains of volcanoes. As the first volcano grows, it is carried away from the hot spot, and another volcano grows in its place. This process may continue for tens or even hundreds of millions of years, creating lines of volcanoes linked like the posts in a fence. Eventually, the plate may carry the hot-spot volcanoes to a subduction zone, where they are pulled back into the mantle and destroyed. Sometimes a hot spot beneath an ocean ridge can create a concentration of volcanoes in a rift valley. That was how Iceland was formed in the North Atlantic.

Hot spots can occur almost anywhere. They can create undersea mountain ranges, oceanic islands, or continental volcanoes, and the resulting volcanic chains may cross sea or land. In addition to Iceland, hot spots formed the Hawaiian and Galápagos islands in the Pacific Ocean, Réunion Island in the Indian Ocean, and the Yellowstone plateau in the United States.

HOT-SPOT REMNANTS

The spectacular Glasshouse Mountains in Queensland, Australia, are the remains of an old continental hot-spot chain. Twenty-five million years of wear and tear have eroded the softer rock, leaving only the hard cores of lava that filled the volcanoes' vents.

Coral atolls

Eroded, extinct volcanoes

Active "shield" volcano above hot spot

New volcano forming

Magma chamber

Feeder channel

Mantle melting in thermal plume

Word Builders

• Hot spots usually form low, wide volcanoes. These are known as **shield volcanoes** because, especially from above, they look like the shields that warriors once used in battle.
• An **atoll** is a coral island that encircles a lagoon. "Atoll" comes from *atolou,* a word used for this type of island in the Maldives in the Indian Ocean.

That's Amazing!

• Measured from seafloor to peak, hot-spot volcano Mauna Loa on Hawaii is the world's tallest mountain. It is nearly 6 miles (over 9 km) high— far taller than Mount Everest, the tallest mountain on land.
• A hot spot now under Marion Island in the southern Indian Ocean has been erupting for almost 185 million years.

Pathfinder

• Scientists now think that hot patches on the outside of Earth's core may be the source of hot spots. Learn about the core on pages 8–9.
• Vast hot-spot lava flows, called flood basalts, cover huge areas of the globe. Find out more on pages 48–49.

THE HOT-SPOT CYCLE

This diagram illustrates the birth, life, and death of hot-spot volcanoes. At the front, active volcanoes are erupting above the hot spot. Behind lie older volcanoes that have been worn down by erosion. Those whose rims are fringed with coral are called atolls. Those that lie underwater are called seamounts. The oldest seamounts are sliding into a subduction trench, slowly returning to Earth's fiery interior.

Seamount

Continental plate

Subduction zone

Direction of plate movement

Oceanic plate

THE LINKS IN THE CHAIN

When magma first bursts through a plate, so much lava floods out that, within a million years, it may be deeper than the Grand Canyon and wider than Greenland. But then the flow eases and smaller volcanoes form.

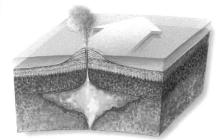

First, a single volcano forms above the hot spot, growing in size as the lava builds up. However, as the plate moves, it carries the volcano away from the hot spot.

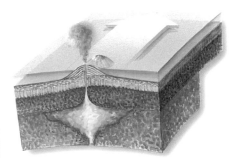

After millions of years, the volcano separates from the hot spot, its lava supply is cut off, and it becomes extinct. A new active volcano then forms above the hot spot.

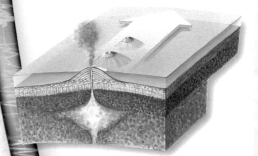

In this way, the chain of volcanoes continues to grow in the direction of the plate movement. But if the hot spot fades, the chain of volcanoes stops growing.

HANDS ON
Homemade Hot Spot

❶ Take a large sheet of cardboard and punch a line of four or five holes in it.

❷ Ask a friend to hold a tube of toothpaste under the first hole and squeeze gently. As your friend squeezes the tube, slowly move the cardboard so that the other holes pass over the tube. Watch what happens.

As you move the holes over the tube, a line of blobs appears on the card. These are your hot-spot volcanoes. The toothpaste seeps through the cardboard in the same way that magma bursts through a plate to form hot-spot volcanoes.

Earthquakes

AS PLATES MOVE, some rocks are pulled apart and others are pushed together. Strain builds up in the rocks until they suddenly crack and shift. This sudden movement creates vibrations that travel through the ground. We call these vibrations earthquakes. Earthquakes shake the ground up and down and from side to side. Large quakes can cause severe damage and claim many lives. Because of this, scientists called seismologists study earthquakes to try to understand their causes. From these studies, seismologists have learned a great deal about Earth's crust and its interior. But so far, they are unable to predict when an earthquake will occur.

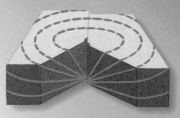
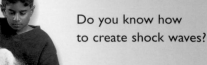

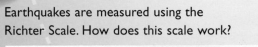
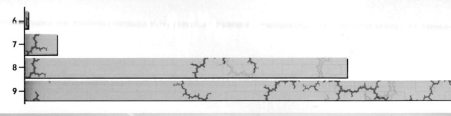

FOCAL POINTS

An earthquake's hypocenter may be tens of miles underground. The strength, or intensity, of earthquake waves decreases as the waves move outward from the epicenter.

Epicenter

Hypocenter

On Shaky Ground

YOU ARE AT HOME, sitting on the sofa, watching TV. Suddenly, you feel the sofa move. You notice the lights swinging and the windows rattling. Objects fall off shelves. You feel like you are on a boat at sea. Fortunately, the movement ceases after a few minutes, and calm returns.

You have just experienced an earthquake. Hundreds of tremors like this shake different parts of the world every day, and many people have experienced them. Fewer, less fortunate people have found themselves at the center of a major quake. This can be a terrifying experience. Inside buildings, ceilings collapse, furniture is tossed around, and windows shatter. Outside, the ground heaves violently. Trees and telephone poles fall. Pipes, drains, and electrical wiring are torn apart.

Just how badly a quake hits depends on its magnitude, how deep it is, and its distance from you. The hypocenter is where the quake begins, usually when rocks suddenly shift along a fault line. The epicenter is the point on Earth's surface directly above the hypocenter. As shock waves spread out from here, they decrease in strength. So, the farther you are from the epicenter, the better. The effects of the quake also depend on the type of ground it hits. Strong bedrock resists shaking, but soft, loose ground shakes violently and may even turn into a muddy liquid, a process called liquefaction.

OFF TRACK
The sideways movement of earthquake waves often shows up in railroad tracks. These tracks in Kobe, Japan, were buckled by snaking surface waves after the main shock waves passed through during a major earthquake in 1995.

THE MERCALLI SCALE
In 1883, Italian scientist Giuseppe Mercalli created a 12-point scale for measuring earthquakes. It is based on the observed effects of a tremor on buildings and people.

LEVELS 1-3
At level 1, the lowest level, tremors go unnoticed. At level 2, people sleeping on upper stories feel movement. At level 3, hanging objects start to swing.

LEVELS 4-5
At level 4, objects rattle and standing cars rock. At level 5, everyone feels the movement, liquids slosh, pictures move, and doors swing.

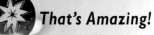

Word Builders

• **Hypocenter,** which is where a quake begins beneath Earth's surface, comes from the Greek *kentres,* meaning "center or location," and the prefix *hypo,* meaning "under." **Epicenter,** which is the point on Earth's surface directly above the hypocenter, comes from *kentres* and the prefix *epi,* meaning "over."
• **Tremor** is from the Latin *tremoris,* meaning "a trembling or quaking."

That's Amazing!

The biggest earthquakes of all were caused by giant meteorites that struck our planet. One collision 65 million years ago in the Yucatán Peninsula may have caused the extinction of dinosaurs. This bang was so big that a giant shock wave rippled right through Earth.

Pathfinder

• The trouble isn't over when the shaking stops. Find out about the aftereffects of quakes on pages 24–25.
• No one can say for certain when a quake is going to occur. But by studying ground movements, scientists can warn if one is likely. Go to pages 26–27.
• Major quakes have devastated many parts of the globe. Find out where and when the biggest tremors have occurred on pages 30–31.

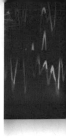

QUAKE!

Major earthquakes are most destructive when they occur near densely populated cities. Most of the danger comes from falling buildings. But bridges and freeways can also collapse, killing drivers and passengers. Broken gas pipes and electrical wires can set off dangerous fires. Outside of cities, quakes can also trigger large landslides.

HANDS ON

Shock Tactics

You can simulate seismic waves by using a small table, a hammer, and sand.

❶ Sprinkle a handful of sand on one side of the table. Strike the table about 3–4 inches (7.5–10 cm) away from the sand with the hammer. Watch the sand jump as the shock waves hit it.

❷ Now hit the table about 8 inches (20 cm) away from the sand. The sand will jump, but not so high.

In the same way, the farther away a place is from the epicenter of an earthquake, the less the ground is affected by seismic waves.

LEVELS 6-7
At level 6, walking is difficult, windows break, pictures fall, and plaster cracks. At level 7, people fall over and chimneys crack.

LEVELS 8-9
At level 8, cars are hard to control, walls crumble, and chimneys fall. At level 9, some buildings collapse, the ground cracks, and pipes split.

LEVELS 10-12
Buildings are reduced to rubble, and landslides occur on hills. Rail tracks bend, and pipes are destroyed. At level 12, destruction is total.

After the Quake

MAJOR EARTHQUAKES are followed by chaos, particularly when they strike cities. Emergency sirens wail, buildings crumble, and trapped and injured people call for help. Rescue teams rush to aid the injured. They use cranes to shift debris and sniffer dogs to locate trapped survivors.

Rescuers and survivors often have to cope with aftershocks. These are the additional tremors that follow a major quake. They are caused by the release of pressure still present in the crust after the first jolt. Usually, aftershocks are weaker than the main quake, but occasionally they are even stronger, and they may continue for a long time. For example, the aftershocks that followed a major earthquake at New Madrid, Missouri, U.S.A., in 1811 lasted for more than a year. Some were just as severe as the main quake, and many people had to move out of the area altogether.

In mountainous areas, quakes may be followed by landslides and avalanches, which may cause further damage to buildings and cut road and rail connections. Earthquakes that occur near the coast can trigger tsunamis. These are waves that spread across the ocean at the speed of a jet plane, growing in size as they approach shallower water close to the shore.

OUT OF CONTROL

After a large earthquake, ruptured gas mains often catch fire. Here, firefighters struggle to contain a blaze following the 1994 Northridge quake near Los Angeles, California, U.S.A. If fires like this are not brought under control quickly, they can be devastating.

WAVES OF TERROR

A towering tsunami is a terrifying sight. As the wave reaches land, it collapses, smashing coastal buildings and hurling boats onto land. Often, tsunamis are far more destructive than the earthquakes that caused them.

INSIDE STORY

A Land Transformed

The prolonged aftershocks that followed the 1811 New Madrid earthquake in Missouri, U.S.A., completely transformed the local landscape. Fissures opened up, coal dust and sulfurous fumes from coal mines filled the air, and whole fields and forests disappeared under water. Rivers changed course, forming new swamps and lakes, among them Reelfoot Lake in Tennessee. One of the aftershocks rumbled all the way to such distant places as Washington, D.C., and Boston, Massachusetts. Nearby, in Kentucky, naturalist John Audubon observed that "the ground rose and fell in successive furrows like the ruffled waters of a lake. The earth waved like a field of corn before a breeze." Although there was tremendous damage to land, there were few casualties because the area was not heavily populated.

Word Builders

• **Tsunami** comes from a Japanese word that translates as "great harbor wave." The name relates to the fact that these waves cause little disturbance until they reach shallow areas of water such as harbors. Tsunamis are different from tidal waves, which are caused by powerful tides and hurricanes.

That's Amazing!

• On July 9, 1958, an avalanche that landed in Lituya Bay, Alaska, U.S.A., created the largest recorded tsunami. It was 1,720 feet (524 m) high—bigger than the tallest building on Earth.
• A tsunami as high as a six-story building hit the port of Arica, Chile, on August 13, 1868. It carried a navy ship, the U.S.S. *Wateree*, 2 miles (3 km) inland, leaving it and its crew unharmed but high and dry. The ship never sailed again.

Pathfinder

• After a major quake in 1906, the city of San Francisco in the U.S.A. was almost totally destroyed by fire. Learn more on pages 32–33.
• The New Madrid quake was unusual because it occurred in the middle of a plate. Find out why most quakes occur at plate edges on pages 10–11.
• Japan has suffered numerous quakes and tsunamis. Turn to pages 34–35.

CATCHING THE WAVES

Most tsunamis form when an earthquake occurs offshore, disturbing the seafloor. The resulting waves spread outward at up to 500 miles (800 km) an hour and rise to great heights when they reach shallow water. The Hawaiian Islands in the Pacific Ocean have been hit several times by tsunamis.

In 1946, an earthquake in the Aleutians created a tsunami that destroyed a lighthouse on Unimak Island. The tsunami swept across the Pacific Ocean, arriving five hours later in Hawaii, where waves up to 30 feet (9 m) high killed 159 people, 96 of them in the city of Hilo.

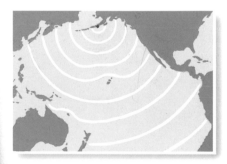

Hilo was devastated again in 1960 by a tsunami caused by an earthquake in Chile. The wave killed 60 people in Hawaii and 120 in the Philippines and Japan. Afterward, buildings in Hilo were moved away from the shore, and work began on the development of a tsunami warning system.

SEISMOLOGICAL RECORD

A seismogram is a visual record of an earthquake. On the one shown at left, the P-waves arrive as close-spaced vibrations. Some time later, the larger S-wave tremors occur. Finally, broad surface waves arrive. These cause the most damage on Earth's surface.

Monitoring Earthquakes

BECAUSE BIG EARTHQUAKES can be so destructive, people have been trying for centuries to find ways of predicting them. The study of earthquakes is known as seismology, and people who study quakes are called seismologists.

In 1876, two Italian seismologists, Luigi Palmeri and Filippo Cecchi, invented the seismometer. This machine contained a pendulum attached to a pillar. If the pillar shook, a pen at the end of the pendulum recorded the tremors on paper. Today, scientists install modern seismometers and other instruments in areas that are prone to earthquakes. They collect and study the information recorded by the instruments at observatories. By exchanging information with scientists at other observatories, they can compare the travel times of seismic waves and their strengths at different points. This helps them to locate an earthquake's epicenter and hypocenter.

By studying these records, scientists learn to recognize patterns that may indicate a buildup to a big tremor. But many factors influence the timing and strength of an earthquake, and even with today's sophisticated equipment, seismologists can only state that a big one will probably, but not certainly, occur.

MONITORING SYSTEMS

In earthquake zones, seismologists position a variety of instruments along the fault line to measure ground movements or other changes that may indicate that a quake is about to take place. Most of the instruments operate automatically and send digital data to observatories via phone lines.

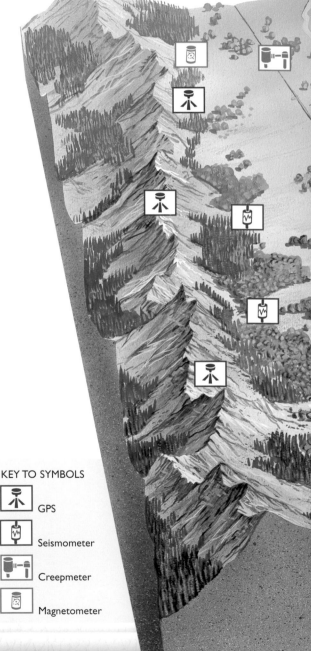

HANDS ON

Tracing the Tremors

You can make your own seismometer and use it to record tremors.

❶ Fill a large jar with water and replace the lid. Place the jar on a roll of paper on a table. Attach a pen to the side of the jar with tape, so that the point just touches the paper. Slowly pull the paper out from under the jar. The pen should make a straight line on the paper.

❷ Keep pulling the paper out, but ask a friend to shake the table gently from side to side. The line will form squiggles like P-waves. Shaking the table a little harder will create larger squiggles, just like S-waves. If your friend then jolts the table from side to side, even bigger, longer squiggles will appear on the paper. These are like surface waves. Now you have your own seismogram!

KEY TO SYMBOLS

GPS

Seismometer

Creepmeter

Magnetometer

P-WAVES

The first waves to arrive during an earthquake are called P-waves, or primary waves. P-waves compress (push together) and dilate (pull apart) the rocks in the ground.

S-WAVES

S-waves, or secondary waves, move more slowly than P-waves. As they pass through the ground, they move rock layers up and down and from side to side.

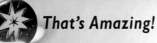

Word Builders

- **Seismology** comes from the Greek word *seismos,* for "earthquake," and the Greek word *logos,* meaning "branch of knowledge." **Seismometer** comes from *seismos* and another Greek word, *metron,* meaning "measurement." **Seismogram** includes yet another Greek word, *grammon,* meaning a "shake" or "line."

That's Amazing!

In some cases, animals have detected earthquakes before they happen. In 1975, in Lianong Province in China, seismologists noticed mice and rabbits leaving their holes and snakes emerging from hibernation. They took this as an indication of an imminent earthquake and asked thousands of people to leave their homes. The next day, a large tremor destroyed most of the province's buildings.

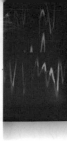

Pathfinder

- Because scientists cannot predict the exact time and place an earthquake will occur, we must take other precautions to protect ourselves. Learn more on pages 28–29.
- Scientists who study volcanoes are known as volcanologists. Find out more about what they do on pages 50–51.

KEEPING WATCH

At a seismic observatory, seismologists gather information from the instruments in the field and monitor it for any significant changes. If anything suggests that an earthquake is about to occur, they warn emergency services.

GPS

Global Positioning Systems receive signals from satellites, which are then transmitted to an observatory. The signals record the exact location of the GPS. A change in its position indicates that the crust has shifted.

SEISMOMETER

Seismometers record vibrations in the ground. Today's seismometers are incredibly sensitive and can pick up even the tiniest tremors. Many, like the ones pictured here, are powered by solar energy.

CREEPMETER

A creepmeter measures ground movement, or creep. It consists of a wire stretched between two rods on either side of a fault. A weight at one end of the wire lines up with a scale. If the fault moves, the measurement changes.

MAGNETOMETER

Earth's magnetic field changes as the strain in rocks varies, so a change in magnetism may warn that plates are on the move. Magnetism is measured using a magnetometer. It can distinguish between general changes and those caused by plate movements.

LOVE WAVES

P- and S-waves are followed by surface waves, which only affect Earth's surface. One type, called Love waves, makes the surface move from side to side like a snake.

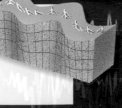

RAYLEIGH WAVES

The second type of surface waves, known as Rayleigh waves, cause the ground to rise and fall like the surface of the ocean when a large wave passes through.

**Helmet and
sturdy boots**

**First-aid
kit**

**Water, canned food,
and can opener**

Preparing for Earthquakes

BECAUSE NO FOOLPROOF method for predicting plate
movements exists, people living in earthquake-prone
areas must always be ready to deal with disaster. Do you
live in an earthquake danger zone? If so, you should
know how to prepare for a quake, and what to do when
the ground starts shaking.

You and your family can make your house a safer place
by securing bookshelves to walls and placing heavy objects
on or near the floor. You can also learn and practice drills and
safety techniques that might save your life during a big
tremor. Lifesaving methods include first-aid, mouth-to-mouth
resuscitation, and fire extinguishing. Breathing from special
bags that are filled with oxygen can help you avoid smoke
inhalation. For people living in earthquake zones, these drills
are as important as learning to swim or cross the road safely.

Governments in places that are prone to earthquakes
can help protect their citizens. They can plan new building
and road developments carefully, making sure that schools,
hospitals, and emergency centers are built on stable land.
They can also make sure that new buildings include features
that make them resistant to earthquakes. These include
strong but flexible steel frames and deep, solid foundations.
Such features can save many lives if a disaster occurs.

Flexible upper
stories

Fire-resistant
materials used
throughout

All equipment
bolted to walls and
designed to resist
upward and
sideways movement

Pyramid shape
has low center
of gravity, which
resists shaking

HANDS ON

Make and Shake

Scientists and architects can see how well new buildings will resist
tremors by building a scale model and placing it on a shake table.
This machine shakes the model just as an earthquake would. You
can build your own simple shake table.

❶ Use a card table, nine medium-size balloons, books, and toy
bricks. Inflate the balloons, but don't blow them up all the way.
Place the table upside down on top of the balloons.

❷ Use the books and blocks
to build different kinds of
structures on the underside
of the table, as shown.

❸ Shake the table legs
gently. What happens? Now
shake the table harder.
Which structures collapse
first? Do some shapes resist
falling better than others?

**Flashlight
and whistle**

**Radio and
batteries**

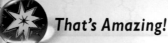

• Preparing for **disasters** is essential in earthquake zones. You can't count on a lucky star to protect you. The word "disaster" actually comes from the Italian word *disastro*, which means "without (*dis-*) a lucky star (*astro*)."
• **Building** comes from the Indo-European word *bheue*, meaning "to be, exist, or grow." The Old English verb form *byldan* meant "to construct a house," but eventually the meaning grew to include any structure.

• Two similar-size quakes hit Armenia in 1988 and San Francisco, U.S.A., in 1989. The Armenian quake killed 25,000 people. In California, only 62 people died, mainly because of safer building practices.
• Ever since the Great Kanto quake in 1923, everyone in Tokyo, Japan, takes part in an annual earthquake drill. It occurs on September 1, the anniversary of the quake, which caused 140,000 deaths.

• Scientists still can't predict earthquakes, but they can detect warning signs. Find out more on pages 26–27.
• San Francisco suffers frequent quakes because it lies on the San Andreas Fault. Learn about this fault on pages 16–17.
• The 1989 Loma Prieta quake was the largest in California in recent years. Read all about it on pages 32–33.
• Japan is one of the world's most quake-prone regions. Go to pages 34–35.

QUAKE-PROOF

Earthquakes occur regularly in San Francisco, U.S.A., so many of the city's buildings have been built to withstand large tremors. The Transamerica Pyramid was completed in 1972 and includes many features that help it absorb or resist shaking. During the 1989 Loma Prieta earthquake, the Pyramid shook for more than a minute and swayed one foot (0.3 m), but remained undamaged.

Emergency stairways built on western wing, eastern wing holds the elevators

White quartz covering reinforced with steel rods, designed to allow sideways movement

Rigid lower floors

20 four-legged support pyramids between second and fifth floors

Deep foundations firmly attached to solid rock move with tremors

BUILT TO LAST

Pagodas are pyramid-shaped temples found in many parts of Asia, with some dating back nearly a thousand years. Their form and structure make them resistant to earthquakes. Normally, the roofs are attached to a rigid central column. This column may sway during a tremor, but it is unlikely to fall down. Furthermore, the roofs can flex up and down without collapsing.

LIFESAVING LESSONS

Japan has regular tremors that are a serious threat to its large population. From a young age, children learn what to do during a quake. In particularly dangerous areas, they routinely practice drills and carry safety gear such as helmets. These children are learning to "duck and cover."

GETTING READY

If you live in an earthquake zone, you should know what to do before, during, and after a tremor.

Make your home a safer place by fastening furniture and appliances to the floor or walls. Keep an earthquake kit handy. It should contain the items shown at the top and bottom of the opposite page.

When a quake occurs, move away from windows and doors. If possible, you should "duck and cover." Duck under a sturdy desk, table, or bed. Hold on tight with one arm and cover your face with the other.

As you move around after a quake, watch out for broken glass, crumbling masonry, and exposed pipes or wires. If you smell gas, quickly ask an adult to turn off the main supply at once.

Major Earthquakes

IN MANY AREAS where people live, an earthquake could strike at any moment. But you're much more likely to feel the Earth move in some places than in others. The shakiest parts of our planet lie at the boundaries of tectonic plates. Along these collision zones, quakes occur regularly as plates squeeze together, scrape edges, and dive beneath each other.

But earthquakes can also occur in the middle of plates, where you would least expect it. Rocks lying along an ancient fault line may suddenly shift. Shock waves from a plate that is subducting at a shallow angle may rise to the surface far inland. Events like this have caused huge tremors in places far from collision zones, such as Charleston in South Carolina, U.S.A., and Tennant Creek in central Australia.

Scientists compare the magnitude, or strength, of earthquakes using the Richter Scale. This was devised in the 1930s by an American seismologist named Charles Richter. The scale has no maximum, but with each step the severity of a quake increases 10 times, and the amount of energy released is at least 30 times greater. Fortunately, quakes of magnitude 8 or more rarely happen. About 1,200 magnitude 5 quakes occur each year. But in the same period, only 115 magnitude 6, 11 magnitude 7, and 1 or 2 magnitude 8 quakes will also happen.

7.4 IZMIT, TURKEY, 1999
On August 17, a sudden movement along the Anatolian Fault caused one of the century's biggest quakes. It reduced thousands of buildings to rubble and left at least 17,000 people dead.

EUROPE

Bucharest, 1977 **7.2**
Izmit, 1999 **7.4**

Al Asnam, 1980 **7.3**

Northwest **7.7**
Iran, 1990 **7.7**

Tabas, 1977

AFRICA

INSIDE STORY
Rising from the Ruins

One of the worst earthquakes in history occurred in Lisbon, Portugal, on November 1, 1755. Estimated at more than 8.7 on the Richter Scale, it hit the country's capital and main port at 9:40 AM. Englishman Thomas Chase described the quake vividly in letters to his mother. He climbed on top of his house to find out what was happening and saw "…shocks of the earthquake, which were attended with a tumbling sort of motion, like the waves of the sea." As he watched, the house collapsed beneath him. Amazingly, Chase survived, crawled from the rubble, and was rescued by friends. He was one of the lucky ones. More than 60,000 lives were lost, and a splendid European city was reduced to rubble.

THE BIG ONES
This map pinpoints some of the largest recorded quakes. Note how many have occurred along plate edges. The main danger zones lie around the Pacific Plate, where it collides with the American and Asian plates, and in southern Europe and central Asia, where the African, Arabian, and Indian plates collide with the Eurasian and Anatolian plates.

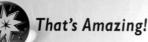

Word Builders

• **Magnitude** is a term for the measured size of an earthquake. It comes from the Latin word *magnitudo*, meaning "size" or "greatness."
• Earthquakes often create large cracks in the ground called **fissures**. The word "fissure" comes from the Latin word *fissus*, meaning "split."

That's Amazing!

• A few earthquakes are so severe that needles shoot off the seismographs that are recording them. One such earthquake occurred in Assam, India, in 1950. It had a magnitude of about 9 on the Richter Scale.
• The 1964 Alaska quake released about 200,000 megatons of energy—400 times the total energy of all the nuclear bombs ever exploded.

Pathfinder

• Discover what it feels like to experience a major earthquake on pages 22–23.
• The tsunami created by the quake in Chile in 1960 killed 61 people in Hawaii. Find out more on page 25.
• Most volcanic eruptions also occur along plate edges. Go to pages 52–53.

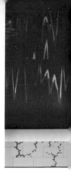

8.2 TANGSHAN, CHINA, 1976

A series of horrific quakes measuring between 7.1 and 8.2 stunned the residents of Tangshan in China on July 28–29, 1976. There were no warning shocks from the earthquake focus, which lay 7 miles (11 km) below the ground. About 242,000 people died.

8.4 ALASKA, U.S.A., 1964

A quake measuring 8.4 hit the city of Anchorage and Kodiak Island on March 27. Tsunamis swamped the harbors, fissures appeared in the land, buildings collapsed, and oil storage tanks caught fire. Miraculously, only 131 people died.

8.1 MEXICO CITY, MEXICO, 1985

On September 19, a quake measuring 8.1 rocked this city of 18 million people. Two days later, an aftershock of 7.6 struck. More than 10,000 people died.

Map labels

Alaska, 1964 **8.4**

ASIA

Tangshan, **8.2** **7.5** Niigata, 1964
1976 **7.2** Kobe, 1995

7.7

Yunnan, **7.6** Taiwan, 1999
1970

7.8 Mindanao, 1976

San Francisco, 1989 **7.1**

NORTH AMERICA

Mexico City, 1985 **8.1**
Guatemala City, 1976 **7.5**

Northern Peru, 1970 **7.8**

SOUTH AMERICA

AUSTRALIA

7.1 Inangahua, 1968

Valdivia, 1960 **8.3**

KEY TO SYMBOLS

Earthquake •

Major earthquakes **7.0** since 1960 with a magnitude of 7 or more (on the Richter Scale)

8.3 VALDIVIA, CHILE, 1960

One of the most powerful series of quakes ever recorded shook southern Chile between May 21 and May 30, 1960. It caused the deaths of 5,000 people, and created an enormous tsunami that swept across the Pacific Ocean.

Fence posts shifted by quake at Tomales Bay, 1906

Freeway destroyed by quake at Northridge near Los Angeles, 1994

California

IN CALIFORNIA, U.S.A., there are tiny tremors every day. Destructive earthquakes rock the state, on average, once a year. Most California quakes are caused by movement along the San Andreas Fault. To the east of the fault lies the North American Plate. To the west lies the Pacific Plate. The Pacific Plate moves slowly northwest as the North American Plate slides southeast. As the plates grind against each other, sudden releases of tension create shock waves.

Since record-keeping began, three massive quakes, or "Big Ones," have hit California—Tejon Pass in 1857 (magnitude 7.9), Owens Valley in 1872 (7.8), and Tomales Bay in 1906 (8.3). The most devastating was the 1906 quake, which destroyed much of San Francisco. More recent shockers include Whittier Narrows in 1987 (6.1), Loma Prieta in 1989 (7.1), and Northridge in 1994 (6.8).

Further major quakes are a certainty. Seismologists estimate that over the next 30 years people in California have a two-in-three chance of experiencing a magnitude 7 or greater earthquake. The state's citizens are therefore working hard to improve their fault monitoring, construct more earthquake-resistant buildings, and expand earthquake education programs. Come the next Big One, Californians will be better prepared than ever.

PORTRAIT OF A QUAKE

In June 1992, a satellite used radar to record a magnitude 7.5 quake centered on the Landers Fault in eastern California. In this image, the black line is the fault. The colored wavy lines show vertical ground movement. The closer the lines are to each other, the greater the movement.

Thirty seconds after the quake started, the shock waves hit San Francisco. A section of the upper deck of the Bay Bridge, which links San Francisco and Oakland, collapsed onto the lower deck, killing one person.

Oakland

San Francisco

In San Francisco's Marina District, houses built on soft, sandy land shook for 15 seconds. Then several collapsed. The sandy soil bubbled like boiling porridge, water pipes cracked, and gas mains caught fire.

ACTION REPLAY

Just after 5 PM on October 17, 1989, a powerful quake jolted northern California. From the epicenter at Loma Prieta, in the Santa Cruz Mountains, shock waves tore north through San Francisco, east to the Sierra Nevada mountains, and south through Monterey. The quake caused $6 billion of damage and killed 62 people.

SCENES FROM A SHATTERED CITY

The most devastating California quake occurred on the morning of April 18, 1906, when a 250-mile (400-km) section of the San Andreas Fault, between Point Arena in the north and San Juan Bautista in the south, suddenly shifted. The epicenter lay 40 miles (64 km) north of San Francisco, at Tomales Bay. In San Francisco, as many as 3,000 people died. About 20 percent of the city's buildings collapsed and almost 80 percent of the city was affected by the fires that followed.

The brick walls of San Francisco's city hall collapsed, and the building was gutted by fire. Only its metal frame remained. A new hall was completed in 1915.

Word Builders

- **Loma Prieta** is a Spanish term that means "Dark Hill." After the 1989 earthquake, the hill was frequently referred to as the "Dark Rolling Mountain."
- In North America, an earthquake is sometimes called a **temblor**. This word comes from the Spanish *temblar,* meaning "to tremble."

That's Amazing!

- Tens of thousands of quakes occur in California each year, but only one in every 10,000 does any damage.
- During the Owens Valley earthquake in 1872, the land along the fault shifted 20 feet (6 m) sideways and rose 23 feet (7 m).

Pathfinder

- In parts of California, the San Andreas Fault appears as a giant scar in the landscape. Go to pages 16–17.
- Find out how scientists monitor earth tremors on pages 26–27.
- Most new buildings in San Francisco are built to withstand large earthquakes. See pages 28–29.

INSIDE STORY

Strike One!

October 17, 1989, was a crucial day for sports fans in San Francisco. A World Series baseball game between the San Francisco Giants and the Oakland A's was due to take place at the city's Candlestick Park. Just before 5 PM, an eager crowd of 60,000 people took their seats in the stadium. At 5:04 PM, the fans suddenly felt their seats shake and saw the floodlights sway. Earthquake! People screamed as chunks of concrete and steel began to fall. But the stadium resisted the shaking. Amazingly, no one was injured. The game, however, was abandoned. Result: earthquake 1, baseball 0.

At the Pacific Garden Shopping Mall in Santa Cruz, shops built on soft river muds swayed wildly and knocked each other down. An old hotel in the mall crashed down onto a department store below.

At the Loma Prieta epicenter, huge cracks appeared in roads, trees swayed violently, and several houses collapsed.

As the seismic waves spread out from the epicenter, the magnitude of the quake gradually decreased.

At Big Sur, entire hillsides collapsed, sending tons of rocks crashing onto the road below.

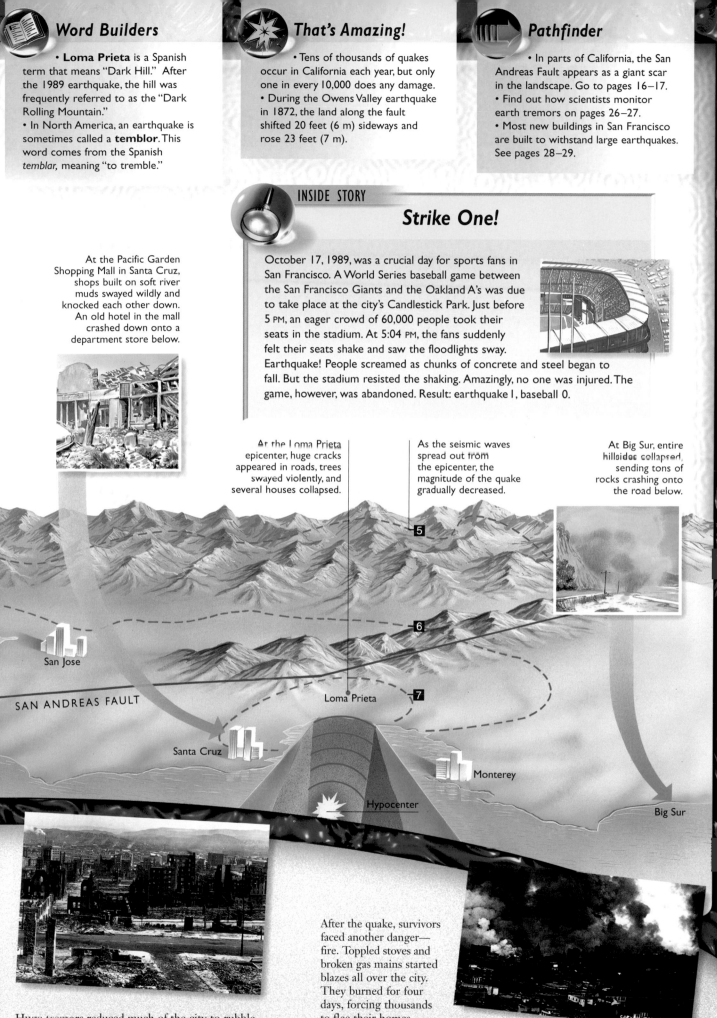

San Jose

SAN ANDREAS FAULT

Santa Cruz

Loma Prieta

Monterey

Hypocenter

Big Sur

Huge tremors reduced much of the city to rubble. Wooden buildings, which are flexible, resisted the shaking better than stone structures.

After the quake, survivors faced another danger— fire. Toppled stoves and broken gas mains started blazes all over the city. They burned for four days, forcing thousands to flee their homes.
When the water mains broke, firefighters had to bring the blazes under control using seawater.

Mount Fuji volcano

Early Japanese seismometer

THAT SINKING FEELING
Many of Kobe's modern buildings were built to withstand earthquakes. But some built on unstable ground collapsed as tremors caused the water-logged soil to liquefy.

Japan

UNDER THE ISLANDS of Japan, three of Earth's plates jostle for position. To the southeast, the Philippine Plate slides beneath the Eurasian Plate. To the east, the Pacific Plate dives under the Eurasian Plate and the Philippine Plate as well. As a result of all of this shoving, diving, and sliding, Japan's 125 million inhabitants experience regular earthquakes, volcanic eruptions, and tsunamis.

Most of the country's quakes are caused by movement along faults that spread outward from the subduction zones. Others are due to volcanic activity. The largest quakes (magnitude 8 to 8.5) occur offshore and in central southern Japan. The far north is the country's safest region, as earthquakes here rarely reach magnitudes of 6.5 to 7.

The Japanese have kept records of earthquakes for about 2,000 years. Ancient Japanese legends suggested that Earth's tremors were caused by the thrashing of a giant catfish (the *namazu*) that lived underground. Today, Japanese seismologists use the latest technology to monitor plate movements and computer models to predict quakes. They also operate highly effective public education programs and one of the world's best earthquake observation networks.

INSIDE STORY
As It Happened

In June 1948, American photographer Carl Mydans was working in Fukui, Japan. Shortly after he arrived in the city, a magnitude 7.3 quake struck while he was eating dinner. "The concrete floor just exploded. Tables and dishes flew into our faces and we were all hurled into a mad dance, bouncing about like popping corn." Mydans rushed outside with his camera. He photographed buildings as they collapsed, and survivors "pinned in their homes." Shocked by the disaster, which killed 3,500 people, he campaigned for the Japanese government to supply every household with an earthquake kit, containing an ax, a crowbar, and a pair of wirecutters.

A RUDE AWAKENING
At 5:46 AM on January 17, 1995, the citizens of Kobe were shaken from their beds by a magnitude 7.2 earthquake. The tremors destroyed 150,000 buildings and left more than 5,000 people dead. A long section of the Hanshin Expressway toppled over as concrete supports gave way.

IN THE HOT SEAT
Japan sits on the edge of the Pacific Plate. As this plate moves northwest, it crashes into several other plates, forming a chain of volcanoes and earthquake-prone lands called the Ring of Fire, shown here in red. The Ring includes more than half the world's volcanoes and causes more than half the world's earthquakes.

EURASIAN PLATE

PACIFIC PLATE

Fukui •   • Tokyo
Kobe •   ▲
  Mt. Fuji

PHILIPPINE PLATE

Word Builders

In Japanese legend, as long as the god Kashima keeps the **namazu**, or giant catfish, pinned down with a large stone, Japan is safe. But if Kashima allows the catfish to escape, it thrashes around and the ground trembles. Throughout history, artists have painted images of the catfish. These pictures, called **namazu-e**, are meant to bring good luck. They often have text that is supposed to cheer up earthquake survivors.

That's Amazing!

• Japan has 1,500 active faults. These have caused more than 400 major quakes in the last 1,000 years.
• On June 15, 1896, a tsunami struck southern Japan, demolishing coastal towns and killing 27,000 people. The wave passed undetected under a fleet of fishing boats out at sea. The fishermen returned to find their homes destroyed.

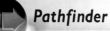
Pathfinder

• Subduction occurs as a thick plate forces a thinner plate down into the mantle. Learn more on pages 14–15.
• From an early age, Japanese children are shown how to protect themselves during earthquakes. Find out what they learn on page 29.
• To learn about major eruptions of some of Japan's active volcanoes, turn to pages 52–53.

FUELING THE FLAMES
Many of Kobe's traditional wooden houses caught fire, and more than 500 blazes flared up across the city.

DOUBLE TROUBLE
Both the Pacific Plate and the Philippine Plate subduct under Japan. The Pacific Plate moves at a rate of 4 inches (10 cm) per year and has dragged the ocean crust 325 miles (523 km) under the land. The Philippine Plate moves at half that speed and has sunk the seafloor 90 miles (145 km) below Japan. This double subduction front gives rise to many of Japan's earthquakes and volcanoes.

ON GUARD
Japan has many monitoring stations like this one. As soon as they detect a quake or eruption, they alert emergency services and disaster control centers.

Volcanoes

WHEN HEAT WITHIN Earth melts rocks, a hot, gooey liquid called magma forms. This liquid rises to the surface and bursts through weak zones in the crust, creating volcanoes. Every day, at every moment, a volcano is erupting somewhere in the world. Large or unexpected eruptions can be extremely dangerous and cause widespread destruction and loss of life. The main threats come from red-hot lava, poisonous gases, and clouds of ash. But eruptions can also trigger mudflows, avalanches, and floods. Because volcanoes are so destructive, volcanologists—the scientists who study volcanoes—try to determine when and how they might erupt.

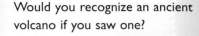

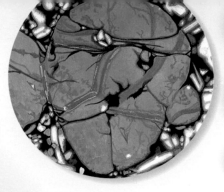

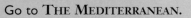

Mount Etna, Italy　　*Anak Krakatau, Indonesia*

Under the Volcano

FROM AFAR, a volcanic eruption may look exciting, even beautiful. But close up it is terrifying. You wouldn't want to be nearby when one occurs. So what are the signs that warn of an eruption? Often the ground rumbles, swells, and cracks. Gas seeps out of holes, and the stench of sulfur fills the air. Showers of rock spray out of pits in the ground, and lava oozes out of cracks. Hot springs bubble furiously. Animals become agitated—when they start leaving, so should you.

A small eruption may consist of little more than a belch of gas. But sometimes the gas throws up molten rock, creating a spray of lava like a fireworks display. As the pressure eases, the spray may dwindle to a steady stream of lava. Occasionally, if lava blocks the vent and a great deal of gas has built up beneath it, the eruption may hurl huge lumps of rock, giant blobs of lava, and vast amounts of dust and ash into the air.

Some eruptions are over in hours. Others continue for tens of years. Many are devastating. Torrents of lava or surges of pulverized rocks destroy everything in their path. Flying rocks can kill, and even gently falling ash and cinders can quickly bury plants, people, and buildings. Within hours, a volcano can transform a lush and lively landscape into a barren desert.

WEATHER PATTERNS
Volcanoes can make their own weather. Warm dust and gases create humid conditions that are ideal for thunderstorms. As a result, eruptions are often accompanied by dramatic displays of lightning.

INSIDE STORY
Diary of a Volcano

In late 1943, Masao Mimatsu, a postmaster at Subetsu in southern Hokkaido, Japan, felt tremors coming from a nearby volcano called Usu. Soon after, he noticed a new dome on the side of Usu. Intrigued, he began to make daily sketches of the new hill, which was called Showa-Shinzan. By the time the volcano stopped growing in September 1945, Mimatsu had a thick wad of sketches that provided one of the most complete records of an eruption ever made. The sketches have now been published in a book. If you flip its pages, Showa-Shinzan rises before your eyes.

Sept. 10, 1945

June 5, 1944

Fissure

Dike: a vertical channel of magma

Lava flow from side vent

Laccolith: a mass of magma that pushes rock layers upward

Sill: a sheet of magma that forms between layers of rock

CURTAINS OF FIRE
Long, vertical cracks in the crust are called fissures. When lava erupts through a fissure, it may form a spectacular red curtain. Fissures can stretch up to 17 miles (27 km) and eject enormous amounts of lava.

Word Builders

• When a volcano is erupting, it is said to be **active**. If it hasn't erupted for a long time but still shows signs of activity, it is said to be **dormant**. If no activity has occurred for thousands of years, the volcano is defined as **extinct**.
• The word **volcano** comes from the name of the Roman god of fire, Vulcan. He was said to live inside a crater on the island of Vulcano in Italy.

That's Amazing!

In February 1943, Dionisio Pulido, a farmer living at Paricutín in Mexico, heard strange rumblings in one of his fields. A few weeks later, he noticed smoke emerging from a hole. Next day, an ash cone 25 times his height covered the hole. A week later, a volcano as tall as a 40-story building covered the entire field. By September 1944, lava from the volcano had buried Dionisio's village.

Pathfinder

• Many volcanoes form above subduction zones. Turn to pages 14–15.
• Vulcanian, Plinian, and Peléean eruptions can all produce avalanches of rocks and ash called pyroclastic flows. Learn more on pages 42–43.
• The danger hasn't passed when the eruption stops. Go to pages 44–45.
• Which were the largest eruptions in history? Find out on pages 52–53.

ANATOMY OF A VOLCANO

During an eruption, lava rushes up to the surface. Some erupts through vents and fissures, but some may remain underground, where it pushes into rock layers. These bodies of magma have different names, depending on their shape.

Ash cloud

Lava erupts through crater

Pyroclastic flow: torrent of hot lava, ash, and gas

Lava rises through central vent

Extinct magma chamber

Magma rises from pool of molten rock called magma chamber

TYPES OF ERUPTIONS

Scientists use the following names to classify different kinds of eruptions.

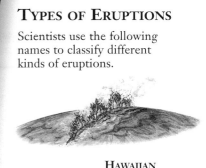

HAWAIIAN
Fountains and rivers of lava erupt from the crater, vents, and fissures. The lava flows create wide, low shield volcanoes.

STROMBOLIAN
Explosions in partly congealed lava throw rock, ash, and cinders into the air. Falling fragments build tall cones, which may collapse if they become too steep.

VULCANIAN
Violent explosions fire large rocks and lava bombs high into the air. These big blasts occur as a result of a buildup of gas under thick, sticky lava.

PLINIAN
These large explosions empty the volcano's magma chambers and produce immense clouds of ash that may rise 30 miles (48 km) high.

PELÉEAN
A dome of hard lava in the crater collapses, releasing a pyroclastic flow. Rising gases form ash clouds above the flow.

Pumice

Obsidian

Lava bomb

Lava Flows

LAVA IS THE LIFEBLOOD of every eruption. It fuels and builds all volcanoes, whether they are located above collision zones, in rift valleys, on ocean ridges, or over hot spots. But its form varies, depending on the chemicals and gases it contains and the kind of eruption that occurs. Explosive eruptions emit thick, sticky lava that either shoots out as cannonball-like "bombs" or flows slowly, like molasses. Less violent eruptions release streams of runny lava that can travel up to 100 miles (160 km), at speeds of up to 30 miles (48 km) per hour.

As lava flows, it cools and solidifies. Volcanologists use different names to describe the ways in which lava cools. Most of these names come from Hawaii, where there are many volcanoes. Lava that forms a smooth or flowing surface is called pahoehoe. Lava that hardens into sharp lumps is called a'a. Thin strands of lava are called Pelé's hair, for the Hawaiian goddess of volcanoes. Solid droplets are known as Pelé's tears.

Runny lava usually cools to form a rock called basalt. Thicker, sticky lava forms other kinds of rock, such as rhyolite. As gases bubble out of cooling lava, holes form in the rock. Gas-rich forms of basalt and rhyolite are called scoria and pumice. Lava that cools immediately forms volcanic glass. This is called tachylyte if it is a basalt lava, or obsidian if it is rhyolite.

RIVERS OF FIRE

During Hawaiian eruptions, runny lava rises directly from the crater or from vents or fissures. It rushes down the slopes, pouring over ledges and cliffs, and filling valleys. The outside surface of the lava flow is the first part to cool. Sometimes the top and sides solidify, forming a tube through which red-hot lava continues to flow.

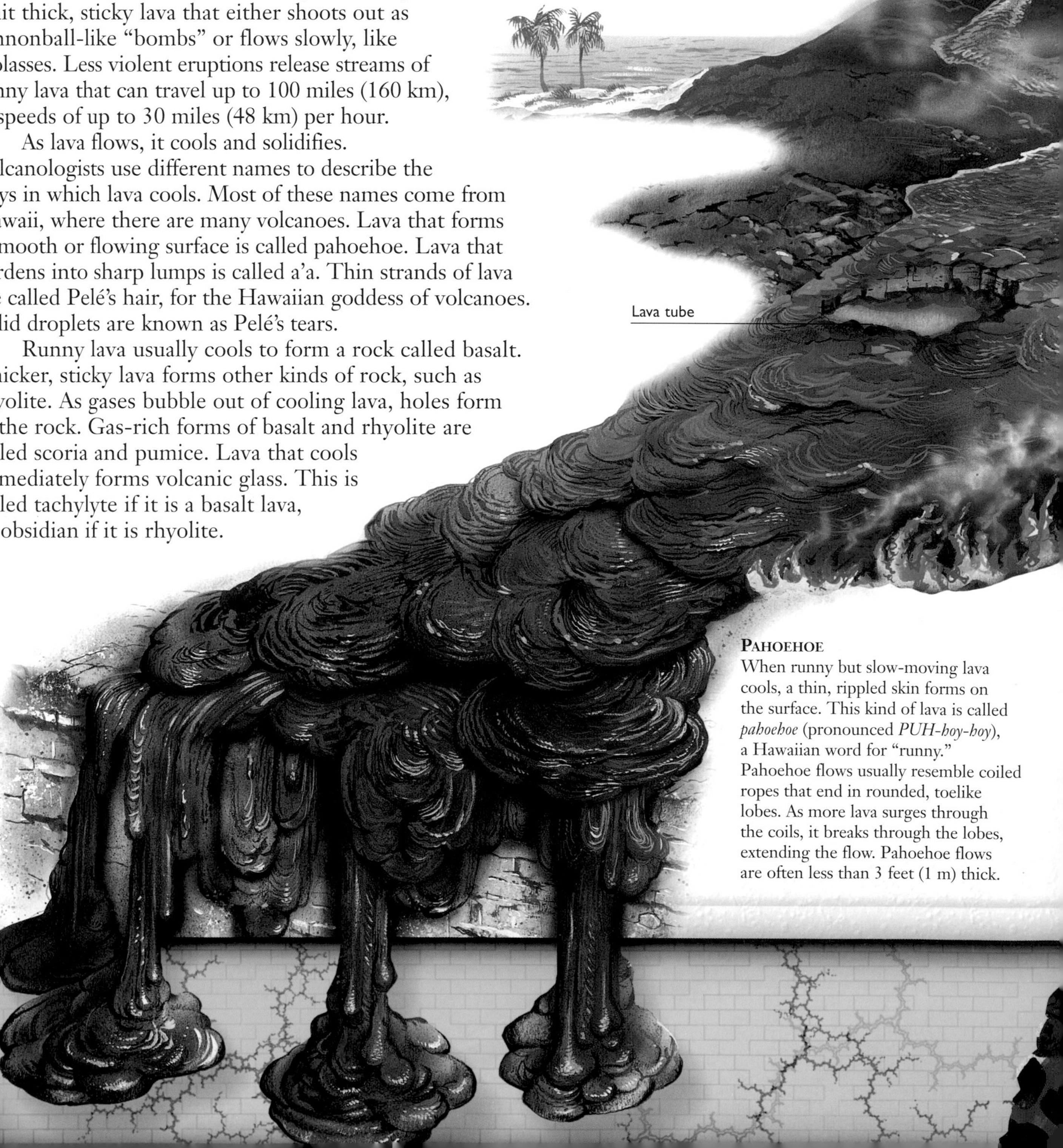

Lava tube

PAHOEHOE

When runny but slow-moving lava cools, a thin, rippled skin forms on the surface. This kind of lava is called _pahoehoe_ (pronounced _PUH-hoy-hoy_), a Hawaiian word for "runny." Pahoehoe flows usually resemble coiled ropes that end in rounded, toelike lobes. As more lava surges through the coils, it breaks through the lobes, extending the flow. Pahoehoe flows are often less than 3 feet (1 m) thick.

Word Builders

• Certain kinds of lava are named after the Hawaiian goddess of volcanoes, **Pelé**. She is said to live inside Kilauea volcano on the Big Island of Hawaii, U.S.A. When she is in a bad mood, she flings lava out of the crater.
• **A'a** is a Hawaiian word meaning "sharp." It is said to come from the sound you would make if you walked barefoot over this jagged rock!

That's Amazing!

• Between 1983 and 1989, Kilauea volcano in Hawaii produced enough lava to make a road that would circle Earth four times.
• The longest known lava flow came from a volcano that erupted 190,000 years ago at Undara in northeastern Australia. It stretched for more than 100 miles (160 km), and its lava tubes are still visible.

Pathfinder

• Under oceans, erupting lava cools quickly to form mounds called pillow lava. Go to pages 12–13.
• The Hawaiian Islands were formed by an erupting hot spot. Find out about hot spots on pages 18–19.
• Lava may spurt out of craters, spray out of fissures, or trickle out of vents. Learn about different kinds of eruptions on page 39.
• Vast, ancient lava flows cover large parts of the globe. Turn to pages 48–49.

ISLANDS THAT GROW

In Hawaii, lava flows often reach the sea. As the red-hot liquid enters the water, huge clouds of steam billow upward. The lava cools quickly and turns into rock, adding new land to the shore.

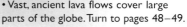

HANDS ON

Make a Lava Flow

① Take 1 cup of self-rising flour, ½ cup of sugar, 2 heaping tablespoons of cocoa, ½ cup of milk, 2 tablespoons of butter, and ½ teaspoon of salt. Mix the ingredients to form a batter. Pour the batter into a greased cake pan. With your hands, shape the mixture to form a slight peak.

② Mix ½ cup of brown sugar with 2 tablespoons of cocoa and sprinkle it on top of the batter. Carefully pour 1 cup of very hot water over the mixture.

③ Place the cake pan in an oven, preheated to 400°F (220°C). Bake for 30–40 minutes. The cake is ready when the chocolate "lava" starts to flow. Remember, lava is very hot—so wait for it to cool before you try to eat it!

A'A

When a large amount of lava erupts quickly, it cools to form rough lumps called *a'a* (pronounced *AH-ah*). This creates a jagged surface, across or under which fresh lava may flow for some time. Eventually, the entire flow solidifies into a massive rock. If an a'a flow fills a deep valley, it may be up to 330 feet (100 m) thick.

PELÉ'S HAIR

Blobs of lava may be torn into thin strands by the wind or by the force of a volcanic explosion. The strands cool as they fall, forming glassy, hairlike threads.

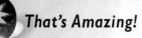

Gas mask　　　　　　　　　　　*Helmet and goggles*

Ash and Gas

ALL VOLCANOES are driven by gas. Some erupt violently when gas is released from upward-moving magma, either because the pressure underground becomes so great that the rocks above can no longer resist, or because the pressure is suddenly reduced by the collapse of the volcano. The gas carries pulverized rocks, blobs of lava, and fine ash high into the sky.

The most common gases in volcanic eruptions are steam (water vapor), sulfur dioxide, and carbon dioxide. Steam can scald. Large amounts of carbon dioxide can suffocate oxygen-breathing life-forms, including humans. Sulfur dioxide can react with water vapor to form sulfuric acid in the atmosphere. Less common gases are chlorine and fluorine, which are toxic and can corrode metals, and hydrogen sulfide, better known as "rotten-egg gas." Wearing a gas mask, helmet, and goggles may offer some protection.

Gas-powered ash clouds can spell disaster. Falling ash may darken the sky for days and cover a vast area. Ash accumulation can clog roads and waterways, buckle roofs, and corrode machinery. Even more dangerous are pyroclastic flows. These red-hot mixtures of ash and gas sweep down slopes at hundreds of miles per hour, destroying everything in their path.

HANDS ON
An Explosive Reaction

Here's a way to see a volcanic eruption without experiencing its bad effects. Make sure you do this experiment with an adult present.

❶ Find an empty squirt bottle and remove the spray nozzle. This container will be your volcano.

❷ Fill the container one-third full of white vinegar mixed with a few drops of red food dye. Place the container in a sink, bath, or open yard. This eruption will be messy!

❸ Now take ½ cup of water, mix in a heaping tablespoon of bicarbonate of soda, and quickly tip the mixture into the container. Stand far back.

A gassy plume will shoot out of the container, just like an explosive eruption. You can repeat the experiment, adding a few drops of dishwashing liquid to the vinegar mixture. This time, when you tip in the bicarbonate mixture, a frothy fluid will bubble out of the container—just like a pyroclastic flow!

DAY TURNS TO NIGHT
In August 1995, heavy ashfalls turned day into night in New Plymouth, the capital of Montserrat. Repeated eruptions continued to rain ash on the city, and finally, in early 1996, it was abandoned. In 1999, the volcano was still erupting and the citizens had not yet been able to return to their homes.

THE MOUNTAIN THAT ROARED
Soufrière Hills volcano on the island of Montserrat in the Caribbean Sea burst into life in July 1995. Steam and sulfurous gas explosions showered ash over the island. Lava domes bulged above the crater rim. Beginning in July 1996, the domes repeatedly collapsed, sending immense pyroclastic flows all the way to the sea. These flows killed 16 farmers. Many of the island's inhabitants had to flee their homes.

Word Builders

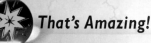

- **Pyroclastic** combines the Greek words *pyros,* meaning "fire," and *klastos,* or "broken." Pyroclastic flows contain fiery pieces of broken pumice.
- **Nuée ardentes** comes from the French *nuée,* meaning "cloud," and *ardente,* or "glowing." Volcanologist Alfred Lacroix first described these pyroclastic flows while studying the eruption of Mount Pelée in Martinique in 1902.

That's Amazing!

- A giant pyroclastic flow released by the eruption of Taupo in New Zealand in AD 186 is estimated to have traveled overland at jet plane speeds of 450 miles (725 km) per hour.
- Pyroclastic flows move so fast that they can skip over water. A prehistoric flow from Kagoshima in Japan traveled 38 miles (60 km), including 6 miles (10 km) over open water.

Pathfinder

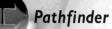

- Ash from volcanic eruptions can combine with rain to form destructive mudflows. Go to pages 44–45.
- The biggest eruptions in history spewed out immense amounts of ash and gas. Find out more on pages 52–53.
- In AD 79, pumice and a pyroclastic flow buried the town of Pompeii in Italy. The town remained buried for more than 1,700 years. Turn to pages 54–55.

PYROCLASTIC FLOWS

Pyroclastic flows are the result of sudden, explosive eruptions. They occur in a variety of ways, but there are two main types.

COLLAPSING VERTICAL ERUPTION

The initial eruption thrusts a huge cloud of volcanic material upward. Eventually, part of the column of cloud collapses and falls back toward Earth. Mixtures of ash and gas race down the slopes of the volcano. These flows can radiate out in any direction from the main vent.

DOME COLLAPSE

Thick lava blocking a vent at the top or side of the volcano suddenly gives way or is blown apart by a buildup of gas. The explosion flings ash, gas, and rocks down one side of the volcano. These pyroclastic flows are sometimes called "nuée ardentes."

GOING WITH THE FLOW

In 1991, a dome collapse at Unzen volcano in Kyushu, Japan, unleashed huge pyroclastic flows that killed 41 people and destroyed an elementary school and 705 houses. More than 8,600 people had to be evacuated.

Aftereffects

LAVA, ASH, AND GAS aren't the only dangers from a volcanic eruption. The aftereffects can be just as life-threatening and are often more destructive. Rain from eruption clouds, snow and ice melted by the heat, collapsing crater lakes, and earth tremors can all trigger landslides and mudflows known as lahars. Lava, mud, and pyroclastic flows may also block rivers, causing flooding. In coastal areas, landslides can, in turn, trigger tsunamis.

Communities affected by eruptions may be vulnerable to other threats. If water supplies and sewerage systems are disrupted, diseases may spread quickly. Blocked roads and railways may prevent medical aid from reaching survivors. And if crops are destroyed, people may starve.

Over longer periods, volcanoes can have a significant impact on the local and world climate. The natural aerosols, or pollutants, pumped out by these giant chimneys spread through the atmosphere. Large, sulfur-rich eruptions fill the air with tiny droplets of sulfuric acid that interfere with the Sun's rays and lower the temperature on the ground. Fluorine and chlorine can damage the ozone layer, a thin layer of gases that blocks harmful rays from the Sun. Eventually, however, the volcanic gases thin out, the climate settles, and the ozone layer recovers—at least until the next big blast.

WASHED AWAY
At 11 PM on November 13, 1985, a colossal torrent of mud engulfed the town of Armero in Colombia, killing more than 23,000 people. The mudflow occurred when a small eruption melted snow on top of the Nevado del Ruiz volcano, 28 miles (45 km) away.

INSIDE STORY

Eyes on the Skies

In December 1989, the passengers and crew on a Dutch airliner flying over Alaska got the fright of their lives—courtesy of a volcano. Ash from an eruption at Redoubt clogged all four of the plane's engines, sending it into a silent dive. It plummeted for 2 miles (3.2 km) before the pilots managed to restart the engines and land safely. The scare forced aviation authorities to consider the threat from volcanic ash. Today, the Alaska Volcano Observatory monitors all eruptions in the northern Pacific. It receives regular reports from American and Russian volcanologists and uses satellites to track ash clouds. In an effort to predict eruptions, scientists monitor seismometers, and carry out regular gas surveys on Alaska's 16 most dangerous volcanoes.

THE YEAR WITHOUT A SUMMER

The April 1815 eruption of Tambora in Indonesia was the largest volcanic eruption in history. About 10,000 people were killed immediately, but thousands more suffered from the volcano's aftereffects, including many people living on the other side of the world.

WIDESPREAD FAMINE
The huge Plinian eruption fired about 1.7 million tons of ash into the air and created enormous pyroclastic flows. The ash fell across a vast area of Indonesia, coating soil and plants and leading to widespread crop failures. As a result, more than 80,000 people in the region starved to death.

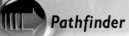
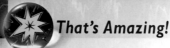
• **Lahar** is the Indonesian word for a volcanic mudflow. Lahars are common in Indonesia, and many volcanologists go there to study these mudflows. This has led to the word being used more widely.

• The word **aerosol** combines two elements. "Aero" comes from the Greek word *aer*, or "air." "Sol" is a substance in which fine particles of one material are suspended in another. In an aerosol, fine droplets and dust are suspended in air.

• In 1982, a jumbo jet passed through an ash cloud above Galunggung volcano in Indonesia. All four engines shut down and the plane dropped nearly 5 miles (8 km) before the pilot was able to restart the engines.

• Aerosols and ash particles from major eruptions can cause unusual atmospheric effects. Colored haloes may appear around the Sun, and as the Sun rises, it may first appear green, then blue.

• The eruption of Mount Pinatubo was one of the largest on record. Find out how it compares with other volcanic eruptions on pages 52–53.
• Learn about the kinds of gases that volcanoes emit on pages 42–43.
• Earthquakes can also cause landslides and mudflows. Go to pages 24–25.
• The 1980 eruption of Mount St. Helens in the U.S.A also produced enormous mudflows. Turn to pages 58–59.

RIVERS OF MUD

The June 15–16, 1991, eruption of Mount Pinatubo in the Philippines killed 320 people and forced 200,000 to leave their homes. But that was just the beginning of trouble. For years afterward, torrential downpours combined with the ash to create enormous lahars. These mudflows killed 600 people—far more than the original eruption. In 1995, one lahar left 100,000 people homeless.

SEVERE WEATHER

Tambora's ash spread around the globe, lowering temperatures in many parts of the world. Some areas of North America and Europe had a particularly severe winter followed by one of the coldest summers ever recorded. As a result, 1816 became known as "the year without a summer."

OPTICAL EFFECTS

Ash particles in the air intensify the yellow and red colors of sunrises and sunsets. After the Tambora eruption, particularly colorful sunrises and sunsets were witnessed around the world. This sunset was painted by the English artist J.M.W. Turner.

Geysers and Hot Springs

THOUSANDS OF YEARS after its last eruption, the area beneath a volcano may still remain hot. In these areas, known as geothermal regions, heat rising from ancient magma chambers encounters water trickling through cracks in the ground. The water deep underground may heat up to 520°F (270°C)—more than twice the temperature of normal boiling water—but the pressure of the cooler water on top prevents it from boiling. However, when water at shallow depths overflows at the surface, the pressure is released and the deeper, hotter water turns to steam and explodes upward. Depending on the amount of pressure, the water and steam may erupt as a giant fountain, called a geyser, or bubble out gently as a hot spring. Sometimes the water and steam rise through soft soil, creating boiling mud pools.

Hot groundwater dissolves minerals in surrounding rocks and carries them to the surface. When the water evaporates, it leaves the minerals on the ground, where they often take on strange shapes and colors.

The most famous geothermal regions are those in Iceland, northern New Zealand, and Yellowstone National Park in the U.S.A. In some places, people use the steam to create electricity and the hot water to heat their homes. For example, geothermal energy, as this is known, provides virtually all of Iceland's power.

KEEPING WARM
Thermal springs bubble throughout the islands of Japan. In the Japan Alps, on the island of Honshu, macaque monkeys have learned to keep warm in the winter by bathing in the hot water.

STEAM POWER
The water in this pool in Iceland comes from hot springs. At the nearby power station, volcanic steam is used to power turbine generators that, in turn, produce electricity.

A HOT-WATER WONDERLAND
Geothermal regions have dramatic landscapes. Geysers spout amid mineral deposits. Hot water drips from terraces. Pools of all sizes, shapes, and colors bubble in hollows. And everything is shrouded in billowing clouds of steam.

Mineral terraces

Mud pools

Word Builders

• **Geyser** comes from an Icelandic word, *geysir*, meaning "to spring up" or "to gush." In Iceland, it is also the name of the country's most famous geyser, which lies 50 miles (80 km) north of the capital, Reykjavik.
• **Geothermal** is made up of two Greek terms: *geo*, meaning "Earth," and *thermos*, meaning "hot." Geothermal activity is created by the hot Earth.

That's Amazing!

• The world's tallest active geyser is the Steamboat Geyser in Yellowstone National Park, Wyoming, U.S.A. Its spout has reached a height of 380 feet (115 m)—higher than a 30-story building.
• The highest-spouting geyser ever recorded was the Waimangu (Black Water) Geyser in New Zealand. It erupted between 1900 and 1904, and reached a height of about 1,500 feet (460 m)—as tall as a 125-story building.

Pathfinder

• The heat that powers hot springs and geysers comes from pockets of magma that have risen from the mantle. Learn more about the mantle on pages 8–9.
• In addition to geysers, Iceland has several active volcanoes and two major rift zones. Find out more on pages 56–57.
• Did you know that there are geysers on other planets? Turn to pages 60–61.

Mineral pool

Geyser

How Geysers Erupt

Scientists cannot be exactly sure how geysers work because they cannot visit the hot underground chambers from which geysers emerge. But experiments suggest that an eruption occurs in the following way:

Surface water trickles down through cracks and a main vent into a cavity. Heat rising from a magma chamber warms the water in the cavity, but the downward pressure of the water in the cracks and vent prevents it from boiling.

As the cavity, vent, and cracks fill up, water eventually overflows at the surface. As soon as this happens, the pressure in the cavity is released. The water suddenly boils, and steam and water rush up toward the surface.

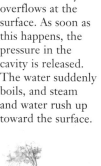

The geyser erupts. Big geysers can spout hundreds of feet high. Some erupt at regular intervals and others are erratic. Once the heat source fades, the geyser will die out.

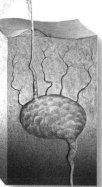

HANDS ON
Make Your Own Geyser

You can make your own geyser with a few simple props.

❶ Fill a bowl with water. Place an overturned funnel inside the bowl so that the narrow end of the funnel rises above the water.

❷ Take a bendy straw and place one end under the funnel. The other end should hang over the edge of the container.

❸ Blow into the straw. Watch what happens.

Water erupts from the funnel—just like a geyser! The pressure created by your breath forces the water upward. A geyser functions in a similar way, although the pressure is created by heat from a magma chamber.

Basalt

Rhyolite

Andesite

Volcanic Landscapes

VOLCANOES CHANGE SHAPE with every eruption. Explosions form new craters, and lava flows add fresh layers of rock. Each event provides a different disguise. Plinian eruptions create the most striking transformations. After these massive explosions empty part of the magma chamber, the volcano collapses, forming a huge crater called a caldera. Domes of lava or new explosive cones may then grow inside the caldera, creating a volcano inside a volcano.

Even after volcanoes become dormant or extinct, they continue to change. Rain, wind, and running water all play a part. Wind and rain scour the rocks, and the rain fills craters. Streams cut deep grooves into slopes. Over millions of years, these elements can erode the volcano's soft exterior to reveal a skeleton of hard lava. This skeleton includes features that originally formed in underground channels and vents, such as plugs and dikes.

Most lava solidifies into basalt, andesite, or rhyolite. Depending on how it cools, the solidified lava may take on strange shapes. Lava that cools quickly in water may form large, pillow-shaped mounds. Some types of lava harden into tall hexagonal columns. Eventually, all lava breaks down into soil that is extremely fertile. That's why people live near active volcanoes, despite the risk of eruptions.

ORGANIC LAVA
These tall columns of volcanic rock in California, U.S.A., look like the pipes of a church organ. They formed when a lava flow cooled. As the lava hardened, it shrank, splitting into regular, six-sided columns.

Plug and dikes formed by lava left in vents of volcano

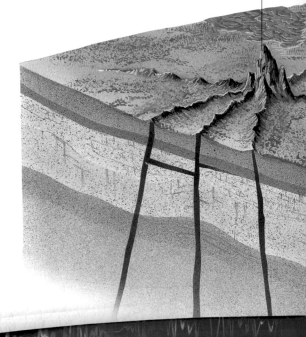

INSIDE STORY
Living in a Fairy Tower

My name is Yashir. I live in Goreme in Turkey. My house is cut into a tall rock spire. The older people call these spires "fairy towers" and say they were once the homes of spirits. But our teacher says they were formed millions of years ago when rivers wore away soft volcanic rock. People began living here about 10,000 years ago. Our house is comfortable. The rock stays cool in the summer and is nice and cozy in the winter. We've got a big living room, a kitchen, and three bedrooms. Recently, my dad decided we needed another room. So he just started digging deeper into the rock.

FLOOD BASALTS
Parts of our planet are covered by deep layers of lava called flood basalts. Most formed when a hot spot erupted and poured enormous quantities of molten rock over the surrounding land. Such events are rare, occurring just once every 10 to 20 million years. Among the most famous examples of flood basalts are the Deccan Basalts in central India.

Deccan Basalts

Réunion

HOT-SPOT TRACES
The Deccan Basalts came from a hot spot that was located below India 65 million years ago. Over the course of one million years, lava flows spread over one-third of India. Large areas of volcanic rock have since worn away, but the basalts still cover one-fifth of the country. Since the original eruption, India has drifted away from the hot spot to its current position. A chain of seafloor volcanoes links the Deccan Basalts to the hot spot, now under the island of Réunion in the southern Indian Ocean.

Word Builders

- **Rhyolite** comes from the Greek word *rhyax,* which means "stream of lava."
- **Andesite** is named for the Andes Mountains in South America. The rock is particularly common in the volcanoes of this long mountain range.
- **Caldera** comes from the Spanish word *caldera,* meaning "cauldron." It is also the name of a crater in the Canary Islands.

That's Amazing!

- The world's largest caldera is Toba volcano on the Island of Sumatra in Indonesia. It measures 685 square miles (1,755 sq. km). Driving in a car at 50 miles (80 km) per hour, it would take you an hour to cross it.
- The Binneringe Dike in Western Australia is more than 375 miles (600 km) long. It would take you two days to drive that distance in a car.

Pathfinder

- Plugs, dikes, laccoliths, and sills were all once channels of red-hot molten rock. Turn to pages 38–39.
- When lava flows cool on the surface, they form types of lava called pahoehoe and a'a. Take a look at these lavas and learn about their names on pages 40–41.
- One of the most famous water-filled calderas is Crater Lake in Oregon, U.S.A. Learn more on page 59.

READING THE LANDSCAPE

Volcanic landscapes preserve evidence of the eruption of lava onto the surface. Jagged rims encircle calderas, and flood basalts show up as extensive tablelands with stepped sides. Highly eroded landscapes may expose the underground channels that once fed volcanoes, in the form of ridges (dikes) and towers (plugs).

LAVA WALLS

A dike forms when magma fills a fissure. If the lava is harder than the surrounding rock, eventually the rock will wear away, exposing a long ridge of lava called a dike. This dike is in northwestern Australia.

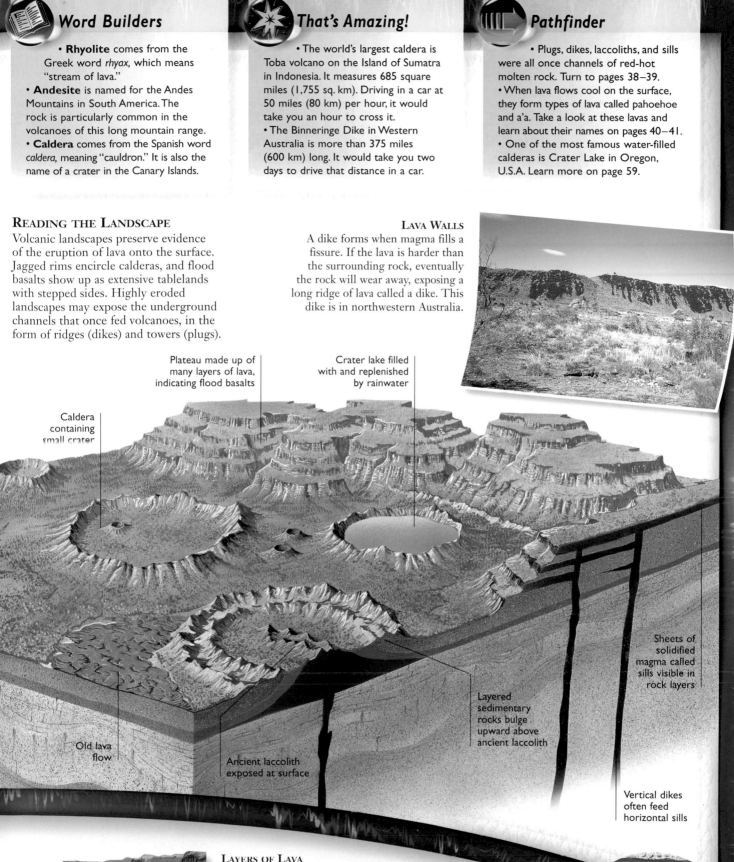

Plateau made up of many layers of lava, indicating flood basalts

Crater lake filled with and replenished by rainwater

Caldera containing small crater

Old lava flow

Ancient laccolith exposed at surface

Layered sedimentary rocks bulge upward above ancient laccolith

Sheets of solidified magma called sills visible in rock layers

Vertical dikes often feed horizontal sills

LAYERS OF LAVA

The Deccan Basalts form large plateaus more than one mile (1.6 km) thick. In many places, rivers have cut down through the volcanic rock, exposing the layers of lava that created the plateaus. Each layer represents a different eruption. The thickness of the layers varies, depending on how long the eruption lasted and how much lava it produced.

CLOSE STUDY

Scientists study the layers in the basalts to learn about ancient eruptions. They have discovered that soils formed on top of some layers before the next lava flow buried them. Sand, clay, and gravel layers between flows suggest peaceful intervals when rivers and lakes developed.

49

Portable seismometer   *Thermocouple*

Volcanology

VOLCANOES HAVE FASCINATED humans for thousands of years. About 2,350 years ago, the Greek philosopher Plato traveled to Sicily to watch Mount Etna erupting, and became the first person to describe cooling lava. Through the 18th century, scholars still disagreed about the origins of volcanic rocks. A group called the Neptunists claimed that many volcanic rocks crystallized from seawater. Their opponents, the Plutonists, argued that all such rocks formed from molten material that came from inside Earth. It was only in the early 19th century that the Plutonists were proved correct.

The scientific study of volcanoes is called volcanology. Today, volcanologists monitor eruptions using aircraft and satellites, and film volcanic activity from afar. To really get to know volcanoes, however, they have to scramble up steep slopes, clamber into craters, and brave the dangers of lava, gases, and landslides. Only then can they collect samples and set up equipment to record tremors and sounds.

Volcanologists work closely with agencies responsible for public safety in a region that might be affected by an eruption from a particular volcano. By studying the volcano's current activity and its history, volcanologists can evaluate the likelihood of a new eruption. Decisions regarding the evacuation of a threatened area are based on this information.

OCCUPATIONAL HAZARDS
As they work, volcanologists must be constantly on the alert for dangers, such as unsteady ground or sudden buildups of lava or gas.

INSIDE STORY

A Dynamic Duo

French scientists Maurice and Katia Krafft are among the most outstanding figures in the history of volcanology. Maurice first became interested in volcanoes at age 7, when he witnessed the 1954 eruption of Stromboli in Italy. By 15, he had joined the French Geological Society and written his first scientific paper. Katia and Maurice met at college. Together, they studied, photographed, and filmed volcanoes all over the world. They took an interest in pyroclastic eruptions because they were "the most dangerous and most deadly." Tragically, at Unzen in Japan, on June 3, 1991, a pyroclastic flow swept the Kraffts and 39 other people away. The world mourned the loss of two intrepid volcanologists, but their important work remains.

Using portable seismometer to measure tremors

Sampling volcanic gases

Word Builders

• **Neptunists** were named for Neptune, the Roman god of the sea. **Plutonists** were named for Pluto, the Roman god of the underworld. These names relate to the groups' views on the origins of volcanic rocks.
• The word **volcanology** is made up of the Italian name *Volcan,* for the Roman god of fire, and the Greek term *logia,* which means "a branch of knowledge."

That's Amazing!

• The seismometers at the Hawaiian Volcano Observatory are so sensitive that they can detect magma rising from Earth's mantle or from chambers in the crust long before it reaches the surface.
• Aerial surveys using ice-penetrating radar have detected active volcanoes buried 1 mile (1.6 km) below the Antarctic ice sheet.

Pathfinder

• Scientists also use seismometers to monitor earthquakes. Find out more on pages 26–27.
• Read about what happens just before and during an eruption on pages 38–39.
• Warning signs allowed scientists to evacuate many people from around Mount St. Helens in the U.S.A. before it erupted violently in 1980. Find out more on pages 58–59.

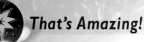

IN THE FIELD

Volcanologists work in teams, with each scientist handling a particular task. Some take the temperature of the lava with a thermocouple. Others monitor tremors with portable seismometers. Those who work closest to the lava wear heat-resistant clothing.

Measuring the size of the crater

Measuring the temperature of the lava

LEARNING FROM LAVA

Scientists scoop up lava on long poles bearing prongs. They study lava samples to learn how volcanic rocks form and what they are made of. They can also find out which part of Earth's interior the lava originally came from.

Some lava flows contain pieces of rock from Earth's mantle, which allows scientists to study rocks they could not otherwise obtain. The green pieces in this lava flow are lumps of a rock called peridotite. They formed 25 miles (40 km) underground.

Volcanologists study thin slices of lava under a microscope to find out which minerals make up the rock and therefore what kind of magma lies under the volcano. This provides clues as to how the volcano is likely to behave.

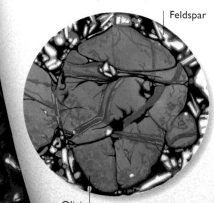

Feldspar

Olivine

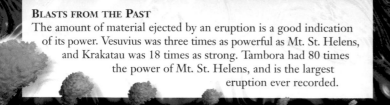

Major Eruptions

THROUGHOUT RECORDED HISTORY, volcanic eruptions have transformed landscapes and affected the lives of large numbers of people all around the world. But some countries have more volcanic activity than others. Most of those countries are located in collision zones—regions where one tectonic plate collides with another. Others lie above hot spots or near major rifts such as the Great Rift Valley in Africa.

Approximately 14,000 volcanoes have erupted in the last 10,000 years. A major eruption is one that explodes with immense power, spews out vast amounts of lava, or causes catastrophic damage. Large explosive eruptions produce an enormous umbrella-shaped cloud of ash and pumice. By measuring the size of these clouds, scientists can estimate the power of different eruptions. They have also used this information to create the Volcanic Explosivity Index, which measures the strength of eruptions on a scale of 0 to 8. Out of 5,000 recorded eruptions, only 160 measured more than 4 on the scale, only 60 were over 5, and just 20 were over 6.

But the size of an eruption does not determine the amount of damage it causes, and even small eruptions can be deadly. In 1985, for example, a small eruption of lava under an icecap on Nevado del Ruiz in Colombia produced a mudflow that killed 22,000 people and destroyed an entire village.

▲ GALUNGGUNG, INDONESIA, 1982
This volcano on the island of Java erupted repeatedly between April 5, 1982, and January 8, 1985, releasing massive ash clouds and pyroclastic flows. More than 80,000 people had to flee, and the homes of 35,000 of them were wiped out.

DANGER ZONES

Like earthquakes, volcanic eruptions tend to occur along plate edges or above hot spots. The greatest concentration of volcanoes occurs in Indonesia—the island of Java alone has 50 active volcanoes. The most dangerous volcanoes are those situated in heavily populated areas such as Indonesia, the Philippines, Japan, Mexico, and Central America.

▲ Laki, 1783

EUROPE

Vesuvius, AD 79

Etna, 1669

▲ Santorini, 1645 BC

AFRICA

INSIDE STORY

Survivor Stories

Only a handful of people lived to describe the eruption of Mount Pelée in 1902. A young girl, Harviva Da Ifrile, was running an errand to a shop on the mountain when the explosion occurred. She saw "boiling stuff" coming toward her, ran to her brother's boat, and managed to sail to a sea cave. Later, she recalled how "the whole side of the mountain…seemed to open and boil down on the screaming people." Auguste Ciparis was imprisoned in an underground cell, which undoubtedly saved his life. He later toured the U.S.A. with the Barnum and Bailey Circus, appearing as "The Prisoner of St. Pierre." Housed in a replica of his cell, he would recount his amazing escape to enthralled audiences.

THE BARNUM & BAILEY GREATEST SHOW ON EARTH

▲ KRAKATAU, INDONESIA, 1883
The August 28 eruption caused widespread devastation. Volcanic material from the eruption clouds crashed into the sea, setting off tsunamis. The waves killed 36,000 people.

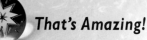

Word Builders

• When Krakatau erupted in 1883, the volcano collapsed, forming a giant caldera in the sea. In 1927, a new volcano rose out of the sea in the center of the caldera. It was soon named **Anak Krakatau**, which in Indonesian means "child of Krakatau."
• **Kilauea** is a Hawaiian word. It means "much spewing," which refers to the many eruptions from this volcano.

That's Amazing!

• The eruption of Krakatau in 1883 was heard 3,000 miles (5,000 km) away and was as powerful as 26 of the largest nuclear bombs ever exploded.
• In 1815, pyroclastic flows surged out of Tambora at the rate of 500 million tons—the weight of 5,000 large ocean liners—every second!

Pathfinder

• Most volcanoes form as a result of collisions between tectonic plates. Turn to pages 14–15.
• Can you imagine what it's like to witness an eruption? Go to pages 38–39.
• Learn more about the eruptions of Nevado del Ruiz and Mount Pinatubo on pages 44–45.

▲ **MOUNT PINATUBO, PHILIPPINES, 1991**
The June 15 eruption killed 320 people, but many deaths were averted—information provided by volcanologists led to the evacuation of 79,000 people before the mountain blew its top.

▲ **KILAUEA, HAWAII, U.S.A., 1983**
This eruption on January 8 eventually became the longest and largest side-vent eruption in Kilauea's recorded history. Lava was still flowing in 1999, more than 16 years later.

▲ **MOUNT PELÉE, MARTINIQUE, 1902**
At 7:52 AM on May 8, Martinique's main town and port, St. Pierre, was engulfed by a white-hot mass of rock, ash, and lava that exploded out of nearby Mount Pelée. About 29,000 people died instantly. Only three people in the town survived.

Bezymianny, 1956

Novarupta, 1912

Mount St. Helens, 1980

ASIA

NORTH AMERICA

Mount Pinatubo, 1991

Kilauea, 1983

El Chichón, 1982

Santa Maria, 1902

Mount Pelée, 1902

Galunggung, 1822

Tambora, 1815

Krakatau, 1883

SOUTH AMERICA

AUSTRALIA

Taupo, AD 186

Tarawera Mountain, 1886

Mount Hudson, 1991

KEY TO SYMBOLS

Volcanic eruption ▲

Major eruption (number on Volcanic Explosivity Index) ▲

▲ **TARAWERA, NEW ZEALAND, 1886**
Tarawera Mountain exploded suddenly on June 10. Villages, hotels, farms, and forests were buried by rocks and mudflows, and more than 100 people died. A famous thermal feature called the pink terraces vanished instantly.

The Mediterranean

DEEP BELOW the sparkling blue waters of the Mediterranean Sea, the African Plate slowly forces its way under the Eurasian Plate. As a result, volcanoes erupt and grow along the sea's northern shore, and earthquakes frequently shake the region. There are two major groups of Mediterranean volcanoes. The first is in southern Italy, mainland Europe's most active zone. It includes Mount Vesuvius, Solfatara and the craters of the Campi Flegrei near Naples, Mount Etna on the island of Sicily, and the Aeolian islands of Stromboli, Vulcano, and Lipari. To the east, a smaller second group of volcanoes stretches across the Aegean Sea and includes the islands of Santorini, Nysiros, and Kos in Greece.

About 3,500 years ago, Santorini was the site of one of the largest eruptions in history. The explosion caused the volcano to collapse, forming a giant caldera that was then flooded by the sea. The most catastrophic eruption since then occurred in AD 79, when ash, mud, and pyroclastic flows from Mount Vesuvius swamped Pompeii and Herculaneum. The towns remained buried for more than 1,700 years.

Mount Vesuvius has erupted many times and still poses a major threat to the city of Naples, which lies at the foot of the mountain and is home to three million people. Although Mount Vesuvius has been quiet since 1944, its every rumble is studied closely. More frequent activity occurs at Mount Etna on Sicily—Europe's most active volcano—where lava flows occur every few years, threatening to engulf nearby towns.

PUTTING ON A SHOW
Regular eruptions from Mount Etna create spectacular, fireworklike displays. Lava flows from the volcano pose a threat to local towns and villages, including the city of Catania (below), located at the foot of the mountain. In 1993, scientists managed to divert a lava flow just before it swamped the village of Zafferana.

PANIC IN POMPEII
At about 1 PM, on August 24, AD 79, Mount Vesuvius erupted violently, raining ash and pumice on the town of Pompeii, 5 miles (8 km) away. Soon afterward, pyroclastic flows swamped the town, burying it under more than 10 feet (3 m) of ash and pumice.

Word Builders

• The name of **Campi Flegrei** near Naples, Italy, combines the Italian words *campi*, meaning "fields," and *flegrei*, for "blazing." It refers to the area's many smoking craters and vents.
• The original Greek name for **Santorini** was Thera. This was the name of a great Spartan leader who ruled the island about 1000 BC. The island was renamed in the Middle Ages for its patron saint, Saint Irene.

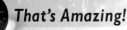

That's Amazing!

Before Mount Vesuvius exploded in AD 79, people living nearby had no idea that it was a volcano, because it hadn't erupted for 600 years. After the AD 79 eruption, Pompeii was so deeply buried that local people forgot it had existed. It was only in the 19th century that archeologists dug up the town and rediscovered its name.

Pathfinder

• Take a look at the plate boundaries that run through the Mediterranean on pages 10–11.
• Find out about major earthquakes that occurred in the Mediterranean region on pages 30–31.
• Ash from a volcanic eruption caused inhabitants to abandon the town of Plymouth in Montserrat in 1996. Find out more on pages 42–43.

INSIDE STORY
Digging up the Past

"I am making you Director of Excavations at Pompeii," said King Victor-Emmanuel II to Giuseppe Fiorelli, in December 1860. Builders working on a canal had uncovered ancient streets and buildings near Naples. The king was excited by the discoveries and hired the archeologist Fiorelli, who was already famous for his scientific studies of ancient coins, to dig up the buried town. Fiorelli devised new ways of excavating the ruins and created an ingenious method for making plaster casts of holes in the ash. He also used the new invention of photography to record his findings.

TIME CAPSULES

The ash and pumice that erupted from Mount Vesuvius destroyed a city but also preserved evidence of the eruption and of the lifestyles of Pompeii's inhabitants. Giuseppe Fiorelli devised the following method for making casts of the bodies of those who perished under the ash.

Thousands of people in Pompeii were suffocated and buried by the huge amounts of ash falling on the city. As the ash piled up, it compacted around their bodies, clothing, and belongings.

Gradually, the bodies decayed, leaving the skeleton, jewelry, and other hard objects inside the cavity. When the archeologists discovered a cavity, they carefully filled it with plaster of paris.

Once the plaster hardened, the ash was carefully removed, revealing a perfect model of the victim. Some of the casts were left where they were found, but some are now on display in museums.

Iceland

ICELAND IS KNOWN as "the land of ice and fire." On the surface it is icy cold for much of the year, but underneath, volcanic fires rage. There are two good reasons for this activity. First, the island lies over a hot spot. Second, it sits on top of the Mid-Atlantic Ridge, a seafloor spreading zone. Together, the hot spot and the spreading ridge produce huge amounts of lava that erupt regularly through vents, fissures, and craters.

The Mid-Atlantic Ridge runs under the middle of the island, from the north to the southwest, forming a strip of rifts and fissures about 40 miles (64 km) wide. Here the land is spreading apart at approximately the rate that your fingernails grow. The hot spot is located under the southeastern part of the island. Krafla, lying on the ridge above the hot spot, has frequent fissure eruptions. The biggest explosive eruptions in Iceland's history occurred at Hekla in 1104, Öraefajökull in 1362, and Askja in 1875. Enormous lava flows followed the eruptions of Eldgja in AD 930 and Laki in 1783.

Icelanders have had to learn to live with dangerous eruptions, but they also benefit from the island's volcanic features. Natural steam heats more than 80 percent of the island's homes, and is used to power turbines that create most of the island's electricity. In addition, the spectacular volcanoes, geysers, and hot springs attract tourists from all over the world.

SPLIT DOWN THE MIDDLE

On Iceland, seafloor spreading occurs on land. As the ocean plates on either side of the Mid-Atlantic Ridge move apart, they push the eastern and western sides of the island in opposite directions. This causes narrow blocks of land to drop downward, forming deep faults like this one near Lake Myvatn in the north of the island.

INSIDE STORY

Halting the Lava

The situation seemed hopeless in January 1973. Lava was advancing across the shore of Vestmannaeyjar, on the island of Heimaey, threatening to block its harbor. Respected volcanologists declared that the island should be abandoned. But physics professor Thorbjorn Sigurgeirsson thought otherwise. He suggested hosing the lava with cold seawater to solidify it. Volunteers used 47 pumps to soak the molten rock. The U.S. Geological Survey called it "the greatest effort ever attempted to control lava flows." Finally, after three months and 6 million tons of water, the lava was halted. Thorbjorn's idea had saved the harbor.

UNDER THE ICECAP

Grimsvötn volcano in southeastern Iceland lies under Vatnajökull icecap, the largest glacier in Europe. In September 1996, a fissure erupted between Grimsvötn and a neighboring volcano, Bardabunga. Hot lava melted a 600-foot (180-m) deep hole in the ice, releasing a billowing plume of ash and steam. The eruption lasted 13 days.

MIXING ICE AND FIRE

Lake Myvatn • Krafla

Vatnajökull icecap

Bardabunga ▲
Grimsvötn ▲

Heimaey

Surtsey

Subglacial water flow

Word Builders

- A **jokulhlaup** is a flood caused by an eruption under an icecap. This Icelandic term includes the words *jokul,* for "glacier," and *hlaup,* meaning "flood."
- **Surtsey** was named after Surtur, a giant described in Icelandic myths. It was Surtur's job to set the world on fire once the gods had no further use for it.

That's Amazing!

- Iceland has produced one third of all the lava that has erupted on land since AD 1500.
- The eruption at Laki in 1783 was the single largest eruption of lava in history. It poured out 3 cubic miles (13 cubic km) of lava—enough to bury a city 15 miles (24 km) in diameter. Volcanic ash from the eruption fell as far away as China.

Pathfinder

- The western half of Iceland sits on the North American Plate, while the eastern half lies on the Eurasian Plate. Find out about plates on pages 10–11.
- Discover how diverging plates form faults and rift valleys on pages 12–13.
- Iceland's volcanoes have produced vast lava flows. Learn about different kinds of lava flows on pages 40–41.
- Did you know that the word "geyser" comes from Iceland? Go to page 47.

A TOWN UNDER FIRE

On January 23, 1973, lava erupted from a fissure near Vestmannaeyjar on the island of Heimaey. Many of the town's buildings were buried under a hail of black ash. Others were demolished by a massive lava flow, which added one square mile (2.6 sq. km) of land to the island and threatened to block the entrance to the town's harbor.

BIRTH OF AN ISLAND

On November 15, 1963, an eruption occurred under the sea off the south coast of Iceland. Explosions threw up billowing clouds of vapor and towering sprays of lava. The lava piled up on the seafloor, eventually forming a new island called Surtsey.

AN ICY TORRENT

That October, billions of gallons of meltwater drained into a crater lake beneath the ice. On November 5, the lake overflowed, creating a giant flood, or *jokulhlaup,* which tore off parts of the icecap.

AFTER THE FLOOD

Water poured out at almost 2 million cubic feet (55,000 cubic m) per second—equal to the rate of flow of the Congo, the world's second-largest river. It carried huge boulders and blocks of ice, which destroyed bridges, power lines, and roads. Luckily, the flood lasted just one day.

Mount Rainier, Washington, U.S.A.

Mount Garibaldi, British Columbia, Canada

Western North America

ALL ALONG the western side of North America, ocean plates press against the continent. This has created two major chains of volcanoes. One extends through California, Oregon, and Washington into British Columbia. It includes such lofty peaks as Mount St. Helens, Mount Rainier, and Mount Garibaldi. Eruptions occur here as the small Juan de Fuca and Gorda plates thrust under the North American Plate. Another chain stretches along the south coast of Alaska. Volcanoes such as Redoubt, Veniaminoff, and Augustine erupt as the Pacific Plate subducts under the North American Plate.

Enormous eruptions have occurred in both groups during the past 10,000 years. One of the biggest, the eruption of Mount Mazama, which occurred about 6,800 years ago, created Crater Lake in Oregon. In 1912, the eruption of Novarupta in southern Alaska filled a huge valley with an ignimbrite—a pyroclastic flow so hot that the ash fragments fuse. This valley later became known as the Valley of Ten Thousand Smokes.

The most dramatic eruption of recent years occurred at Mount St. Helens in May 1980. Although it was a relatively small eruption, the explosion and its effects were recorded in detail, making people all over the world aware of the immense power of volcanoes.

BAKED ALASKA
Alaskan eruptions are usually small to moderate in size. At Veniaminoff, a typical Alaskan volcano, regular eruptions normally produce only columns of ash. Pyroclastic flows occur occasionally, but lava flows are rare.

WARNING SIGNS
Mount St. Helens sent out a series of warnings that it was about to erupt—including earthquakes, small explosions, and a growing bulge on the mountain's north side caused by magma moving toward the surface. At 8:32 AM on May 18, 1980, an earthquake triggered a landslide that removed the upper part of the volcano.

Magma builds up under north flank

Massive landslide triggers eruption through top and flank of volcano

INSIDE STORY
A Bird's-Eye View

On May 18, 1980, geologists Keith and Dorothy Stoffel flew their small plane over Mount St. Helens. They were eager to take a closer look at the volcano, which had been rumbling and smoking since March. As they neared the peak, they suddenly noticed "landsliding of rock and ice debris inward into the crater…The entire north side of the summit began sliding…A huge explosion blasted out." The plane had to make a steep dive to outrun the mushrooming eruption cloud, but the Stoffels made it to safety with some dramatic photos and an amazing story.

Word Builders

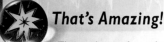

- **The Valley of Ten Thousand Smokes** was named by Robert Griggs, the leader of an expedition sent to investigate the 1912 Novarupta eruption. Griggs named the valley for the many jets of steam rising from the still-hot ignimbrite sheet. Most of the jets died after a few years, but the name remains.
- **Ignimbrite** comes from the Latin words *ignis,* meaning "fire," and *imber,* meaning "shower."

That's Amazing!

- The explosion from the 1912 Novarupta eruption was heard 730 miles (1,200 km) to the east in Juneau, Alaska, U.S.A. But because the wind was blowing eastward, people at Kodiak, 100 miles (160 km) west of the mountain, didn't hear the blast at all.
- The eruption of Mount Mazama blew out 30 times as much ash as the Mount St. Helens eruption.

Pathfinder

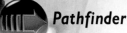

- Most of the volcanoes in western North America were formed by subduction. Find out more about subduction on pages 14–15.
- Crater lakes are just one of many features created by volcanic activity. Take a look at some others on pages 48–49.
- The 1980 eruption of Mount St. Helens was a Plinian eruption. Learn about other types of eruption on page 39.

FLOODED CRATER

The blue waters of Crater Lake in Oregon, U.S.A., fill a deep caldera formed by the eruption of Mount Mazama 6,800 years ago. The island in the center of the lake is called Wizard Island. It is a volcanic cone that formed about 4,670 years ago.

SCENES OF DEVASTATION

The Mount St. Helens eruption claimed 60 lives. Most of the victims died in the initial blast, which traveled faster than the speed of sound (745 miles [1,200 km] per hour). The explosion was followed by avalanches, mudflows, and ash clouds.

The blast snapped, flattened, and stripped trees over an area of 230 square miles (600 sq. km), and killed tens of thousands of animals. U.S. Forest Service scientists predicted it would be a century before the environment recovered fully.

Huge column of ash rises high into the air

Rock, hot ash, and lava roar down the mountainside. Melting snow combines with ash to form mudflows.

The landslide cascaded into nearby Spirit Lake and Toutle River. Lake waters slopped out, forming huge mudflows. These swept down the mountain, destroying houses, bridges, roads, and trees.

Winds carried the ash cloud 930 miles (1,500 km) eastward. It blocked out the Sun in some areas, damaged machinery and vehicles, and caused widespread breathing problems. Although it had immediate effects on Earth's atmosphere, it had little permanent impact on the climate.

Seismograph
on the Moon

Ice geyser
on Neptune

Sojourner
probe on Mars

Extraterrestrial Volcanoes

EARTH IS NOT THE ONLY volcanic body in our solar system.
Several rocky planets and moons, including Earth's own
moon, display traces of volcanic activity—and some have
active volcanoes. Scientists study volcanic activity on other
planets and moons by viewing them through telescopes,
looking at pictures taken by space probes, and examining
space rocks that crash to Earth as meteorites. They've also
studied rocks that astronauts have collected from the Moon.

You can see ancient lava flows on the Moon. They
form large dark patches within giant impact craters. Samples
of moon rocks reveal that these patches are made of a type
of basalt similar to the basalt found on Earth. Some glassy
grains resemble the lava formations known as Pele's tears,
which are found on Hawaii.

Mars has extinct volcanoes, ancient lava flows, and
some pyroclastic deposits. Venus has high shield volcanoes
and large lava flows, some of which may have formed fairly
recently. Farther out in the solar system, Io, one of Jupiter's
moons, is a hotbed of volcanic activity. Its giant volcanoes
spray out huge clouds of sulfuric steam. The sulfur deposits
have colored its surface in shades of yellow and red. Even
the gas giants, Saturn and Neptune, and their moons show
signs of volcanic activity—marks that suggest these frozen
bodies are studded with icy geysers.

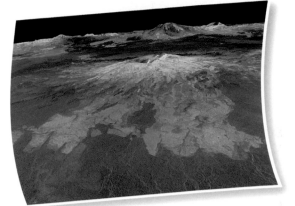

VENUSIAN VOLCANOES
This image was created on computers using
data gathered by the Magellan space probe. It
shows one of the largest volcanoes on Venus,
Maat Mons, which rises 3 miles (5 km) high.
It is surrounded by giant lava flows, which
show up as bright areas in the photograph.

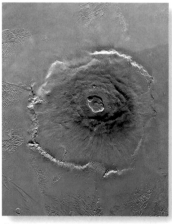

MAMMOTH MARTIAN
One of the most prominent
features on Mars is this huge
volcano called Olympus Mons.
It measures 375 miles (600 km)
across, rises 16 miles (25 km) high,
and is edged by cliffs 2.5–5 miles
(4–8 km) high. All of the Hawaiian
Islands could easily fit inside it.

HANDS ON

Moonwatching

You can take a closer look at the lava plains on the Moon
with an ordinary pair of binoculars. The best time to look is
between the new moon and a full moon, when shadows
make the outlines of lunar features stand out. Use the
picture at the lower right to pinpoint the largest
maria. (Remember that if you are in the southern
hemisphere, the features will be the other way up.)
You should be able to see the dark plains and many
impact craters quite clearly. The Mare Tranquillitatis
is where the *Apollo 11* astronauts landed. Imagine
studying volcanoes up there!

LUNAR LAVA FLOWS

The Moon's surface is studded with huge
craters that contain giant lava plains called
maria. The plains formed in the following way.

CRASH LANDINGS
About three to four billion years ago,
numerous enormous asteroids collided
with the Moon. These impacts formed
large craters up to 900 miles (1,450 km)
in diameter. Shock waves from the
collisions fractured the underlying crust.

Word Builders

• **Maat Mons** was named after Maat, the Egyptian goddess of truth and justice. **Olympus Mons** was named after Mount Olympus in Greece, said to be the home of the gods in Greek mythology. *Mons* is a Latin word, meaning "a towering mass or mountain."
• **Mare** is a Latin word, meaning "sea." On the Moon, a mare is a sea of lava. The plural of mare is **maria**.

That's Amazing!

• Olympus Mons on Mars is more than 20 times the size of Earth's largest volcano, Mauna Loa. Earth's crust would probably collapse under the weight of such a mammoth mountain.
• Io is the size of Earth's Moon, but has 20 times the volcanic activity of Earth.
• The Moon's volcanoes have been extinct for more than 1 billion years, but the lava is still visible because there are no plants or water to cover it.

Pathfinder

• To find out how Earth's internal structure compares to those of neighboring planets, turn to page 8.
• Like the volcanoes on Io, some of Earth's volcanoes expel large amounts of sulfur. This can have an effect on our planet's climate. Go to pages 44–45.
• Huge basalt lava flows also cover parts of Earth, although much of the rock is hidden by water and vegetation. Find out more on pages 48–49.

SULFUR PLUMES

Volcanoes and lava flows pockmark the surface of Io, one of Jupiter's moons. The volcanoes eject umbrella-shaped sprays of sulfur and sulfur dioxide up to 180 miles (300 km) high. You can see one at the top of this photo taken by the Voyager probe.

Mare Serenitatis

Mare Imbrium

RISING LAVA

The fractures released some of the pressure under the crust. This caused large amounts of molten rock to form and rise toward the surface. Gradually, the molten rock filled the craters, forming seas of lava, or maria.

ON THE FACE OF IT

The lava-filled craters appear as scattered dark patches on the face of the Moon. They contrast with lighter-colored upland rocks. Some of the lava plains are thousands of miles wide. Among the largest is the Mare Imbrium.

Mare Foecunditatis

Mare Tranquillitatis

Glossary

a'a A type of lava that has a jagged surface.

active volcano A volcano that produces regular eruptions of gas and lava. The bursts may be separated by weeks or many centuries.

aerosol Small particles and liquid droplets introduced by volcanic gases into air.

aftershock A tremor that follows a large earthquake and originates at or near the hypocenter of the initial quake.

ash Fine pieces of rock and lava ejected during volcanic eruptions.

asthenosphere A layer in Earth's upper mantle, so soft that it can flow. It contains pockets of hot, soft rock.

black smoker A vent situated on an ocean ridge that emits hot, mineral-laden water.

caldera A large, circular depression formed when a volcano collapses above its magma chamber.

continent One of Earth's seven main landmasses: Africa, Antarctica, Asia, Australia, Europe, North America, and South America. The landmasses include edges beneath the ocean as well as dry land.

convection current A current that transfers heat through moving material, such as the movement of hot rock in the mantle.

convergent margin A boundary between two tectonic plates that are moving toward each other.

core Earth's center. It consists of a solid inner core and a molten outer core, both of which are made of an iron-nickel alloy.

crater A circular depression formed as a result of a volcanic eruption (volcanic crater) or by the impact of a meteorite (impact crater).

crater lake A water-filled crater. It may be filled on a seasonal or permanent basis.

crust The outermost solid layer of Earth, which varies from a thickness of 3 miles (5 km) under the oceans to 45 miles (72 km) under the continents.

dike A sheet of igneous rock formed when magma rises through a crack.

divergent margin A boundary between two tectonic plates that are moving apart.

dormant volcano A volcano that is not currently active but that could erupt again.

epicenter The point on Earth's surface that is directly above the hypocenter, or starting point, of an earthquake.

eruption The volcanic release of lava and gas from Earth's interior onto the surface and into the atmosphere.

extinct volcano A volcano that has shown no sign of activity for a long period and is considered unlikely to erupt again.

fault margin A crack in rock layers created by the rocks shifting in opposite directions or at different speeds.

fissure A fracture or crack in the ground. In volcanic areas, a fissure may be associated with a line of vents (known as fissure volcanoes).

flood basalt A flow of basalt lava that spreads over a large area. It forms a basalt plateau.

geothermal energy Energy that can be extracted from Earth's interior heat, whether from hot rocks, hot water, or steam.

geyser A surface vent that periodically spouts a fountain of boiling water.

hot spot A persistent zone of melting within Earth's mantle.

hypocenter The place within Earth where energy in strained rocks is suddenly released as earthquake waves.

island arc An arc-shaped chain of volcanic islands that forms above a subducting seafloor.

laccolith A mushroom-shaped body of volcanic rock formed when rising magma pushes rock layers upward.

lahar A mudflow created by a volcanic eruption.

lateral fault A fault along which rocks have moved sideways. It is sometimes called a strike-slip or transform fault.

lava Molten rock that has erupted from a volcano onto Earth's surface.

lava bomb A large lump of lava, usually more than 1.25 inches (32 mm) across, that is thrown out of a volcano.

lava dome A mound of thick, sticky lava that grows at the top of, or on the flanks of, a volcano.

lava flow A stream of lava that erupts from a volcano and runs over surrounding land.

lava tube An underground river of lava formed when the surface of an open lava channel solidifies.

liquefaction The change of sediment or soil into a fluid mass as a result of an earthquake.

lithosphere The rigid outer part of Earth, consisting of the crust and the uppermost part of the mantle.

magma Melted rock found inside Earth. It may solidify inside Earth or erupt at the surface to form lava.

magma chamber A pool of magma in the upper part of the lithosphere from which volcanic materials may erupt.

magnitude The strength of an earthquake, based on the amount of energy released. Seismologists measure magnitude using the Richter Scale, which begins at zero and has no maximum.

mantle The layer between Earth's crust and the outer core. It includes the lower mantle and asthenosphere—the parts of the mantle that flow—and the lithosphere, which is the rigid uppermost part of the mantle.

mare On the Moon, a dark, low-lying, level, and relatively smooth plain of rock formed when lava flooded an impact crater.

meteorite A piece of planetary material from outside Earth that has fallen through the atmosphere onto Earth's surface.

mid-ocean ridge A long, raised ridge formed by volcanic action at the edges of diverging oceanic plates.

mineral A naturally formed solid with an ordered arrangement of atoms found in Earth's crust.

mudflow A river of ash, mud, and water set off by a volcanic eruption or earthquake. Those triggered by volcanoes are also known as lahars.

normal fault A fracture in rock layers, where the upper side has moved downward relative to the other side along a plane inclined between 45 and 90 degrees.

pahoehoe A type of lava with a smooth, ropelike surface.

pillow lava Lava that forms rounded mounds by cooling quickly after erupting under water or flowing into water.

plug A column of volcanic rock formed when lava solidifies inside the vent of a volcano.

plume A rising column of hot rock in the mantle within which melting can take place. The term can also apply to a large column of ash above a volcano.

primary wave A seismic wave, also known as a P-wave, that compresses and expands rocks as it travels through them. It is called a primary wave because it is the wave that arrives first during an earthquake, before the secondary wave.

pumice A light-colored, glassy volcanic rock that contains many cavities. It is so light that it can float in water.

pyroclastic flow A dense, heated mixture of volcanic gas, ash, and rock fragments that travels at great speed down volcanic slopes. It forms as a result of the collapse of an eruption column or a lava dome.

reverse fault A fracture in rock layers, where the top side has moved upward relative to the other side along a plane inclined between 45 and 90 degrees.

rift valley A wide valley that forms when rock layers move apart and a central section drops downward as a result of normal faulting.

secondary wave A seismic wave, also known as an S-wave, that moves rocks from side to side as it passes through them. It is called a secondary wave because it is the second type of wave to arrive during an earthquake.

seismic Related to an earthquake or tremor.

seismogram A graph or computer image that depicts earth tremors as wavy lines.

seismograph An instrument that detects, magnifies, and records Earth's vibrations.

seismology The study of Earth tremors, whether natural or artificially produced.

shield volcano A wide, low volcano formed by slow, continuous lava flows. This type of volcano looks like a shield when viewed from above.

sill A layer of igneous rock formed when magma solidifies between parallel rock layers.

subduction The process in which one tectonic plate descends below another.

surface wave A seismic wave that travels along Earth's surface. It arrives after primary and secondary waves and moves up and down or from side to side.

tectonic plate Rigid pieces of Earth's lithosphere that move over the asthenosphere.

thrust fault A fracture in rock layers, where the upper side rides over the top of the lower side at an angle of less than 45 degrees.

transform fault A fault or plate margin along which rocks move in opposite directions or at different speeds.

tsunami A Japanese word for a sea-wave produced by an earthquake, landslide, or volcanic blast. It reaches its greatest height in shallow waters before crashing onto land.

vent A pipe inside a volcano through which lava and gas erupt.

volcano A typically circular landform from which molten rock and gases erupt.

volcanologist A scientist who studies volcanoes, active as well as inactive.

Index

The publishers would like to thank the following people for their assistance in the preparation of this book: James Clark, Renee Clark, Richard S. Fiske, Susan Garcia, Malcolm Johnston, Saburo Mimatsu, Doug Myren, William Prescott, Carolyn Rebbert, Tom Simkin, Mary Wilkinson.
Our special thanks to the following children who feature in the photographs: Sienna Berney, Irene Finkelde, Lewis Nicholson, Jeremy Sequeira, and Julian Sequeira.

PICTURE CREDITS (t=top, b=bottom, l=left, r=right, c=center, f=flap, F=Front, C=Cover, B=Back)
AAP Image 22tr, 30t, 31b, 31tc, 34/35c, 37tl, 42b, 53tl. **AdLibitum** 7tr, 7br, 15tc, 17br, 19b, 23br, 26bl, 28bl, 42bl, 60bl (Mihal K). **AKG London** 33br (A.L. Murat), 33bl (Houston & Harding), 53tr. **Ardea** 48tr (John Mason). **Auscape** 59tl (F. Gohier), 54bl (Otto Hahn/Peter Arnold). **Black Star** 31tr (B. Schalkwijk). **Bridgeman Art Library** 45br (Agnew & Sons, London). **Bruce Coleman Ltd** 52tr (A. Compost) **Circus World Museum** 52bl. **Robert Coenraads** 16bl. **Corbis** 57br, 58tr. **Mary Evans Picture Library** 8l, 11tr, 55c. **The Granger Collection** 24bl, 30b, 55br. **NASA** 60tr. **National Geographic Society** 17tr (E. Kristof), 44tr (S. Raymer). **Nordfoto** 9cr (A. Moe). **Oxford Scientific Films** 46bl (R. Packwood). **Pacific Tsunami Museum** 25br. **Panos Pictures** 42/43c (R. Huibers). **Picture Media** 29bc (Kurita Kaku/WADA), 35b (K. Kurita/M.Batsu), 24l (Press Telegram/Liaison), 35tr, 56bl (E. C. Hrafnsson). **Planet Earth Pictures** 53tl (Bourseiller-I & V), 38b, 50c, 50tr, 56c (Krafft-I & V). **Princeton University**/Dept. of Geosciences 12bl. **Rotorua Museum of Art and History** 53b. **Jeff Scovil** 9tr. **Smithsonian Institute** 52bl (National Museum of Natural History). **Tom Stack and Assoc.** 12c (NOAA), 14tr (S. Swanger). **F.L. Sutherland** 49tr. **The Photo Library** 48bl (A.G.E. Fotostock), 9c, 41tr (G. Brad Lewis), 46cl (T. Davis), 38tr (E. R. Degginger), 56tr (R. Halin), 58b (Stewart Lowther/SPL), 32tr (Massonnet ET AL/CNES/SPL), 13r (NASA/ SPL), 43b (S&D O'Heara/PRI), 34tr, 34cl (Sipa Press), 18tr (K. Stepnell), 60cr (SPL), 34bl (US Geological Survey/SPL). **University of California** 31tl. **USGS** 27br, 27c, 27cr, 27tr, 27tl, 61c. **Roger Viollet** 32br. **Wildlight** 15tr (J. Danks).

ILLUSTRATION CREDITS: Susanna Addario 8tc. **Richard Bonson/Wildlife Art Ltd** 4tr, 6br, 6b, 7br, 12br, 12/13c, 12bl, 12t, 13bl, 13br, 18/19c, 18tl, 18tc, 18tr, 19cr, 19tr, 19br, 36crb, 36tl, 37c, 38/39c, 38cl (Mimatsu Masao Memorial Museum) 39r, 46/47c, 46t, 47bl, 47r, 54/55c, 54tr, 54tl, 55tr, 55cr, 63br. **Fiammetta Dogi** 4br, 38tl. **Chris Forsey** 6cr, 6c, 6tl, 7tl, 7cr, 7cl, 8bl, 8tr, 8br, 9bl, 9br, 10br, 10bl, 10tr, 11bc, 14/15c, 14bl, 14br, 14tc, 14tl, 15bl, 15br, 16/17b, 16/17c, 16tl, 16tr, 20crb, 21bl, 21c, 21cl, 26/27c, 26br, 26bl, 26c, 26t, 27bl, 27br, 32/33c, 32cr, 32tl, 32tc, 32c, 33cl, 33cr, 33tr, 34tc, 34br, 36crt, 36tl, 37cl, 37cr, 40/41c, 40tr, 41br, 41cr, 42tl, 43br, 43tr, 48bc, 48tc, 48tl, 49br, 49c, 49bl, 56/57c, 56br, 56tc, 56tl, 56tr, 57bc, 58/59c, 58l, 58tl, 58tr, 59br, 59cr, 59tr, 60bl, 60br, 60tc, 60cl, 61b, 62bl, 62bl, 63tc. **Ray Grinaway** 4tr, 20cr, 20crt, 21tl, 21tr, 22bc, 22cr, 23b, 22tl, 24tl, 24tc, 24tl, 25tr, 25tc, 28bc, 28bl, 28c, 28tl, 28tr, 29tr, 29cr, 29tr, 37tl, 40tl, 44bl, 44br, 45bl, 50tl, 50tr, 51cr, 51br, 51tl, 52tl, 62bc, 62tl, 63tr. **James McKinnon**, 44/45c, 62tr. **Stuart McVicar/Geocart** 10/11c, 11r, 30/31c, 36cr, 44tl, 44tr, 52/53c, 62br. **John Richards** 22/23c, 24/25c, 50/51c. **Michael Saunders** 10tc, 21br, 34tl. **Ann Winterbotham** 10tl.
COVER CREDITS: Richard Bonson Ffb, FCclt, FCtl, Bfb. **Chris Forsey** FCbr, FCbc, Fft, BCbr, BCtl, Bft, BCtr. **Ray Grinaway** FCclb. **John Richards** FCcr, FCbl.

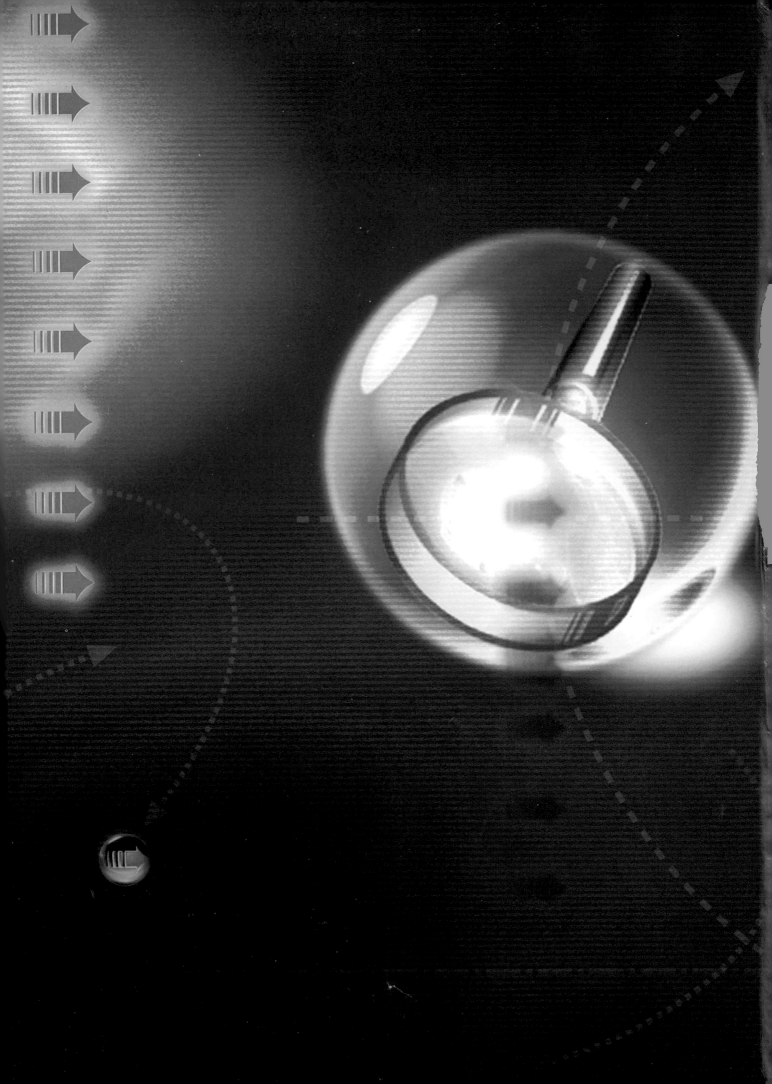